Developing Occupational Programs

Charles R. Doty, *Editor*
Rutgers, State University of New Jersey

NEW DIRECTIONS FOR COMMUNITY COLLEGES
ARTHUR M. COHEN, *Editor-in-Chief*
FLORENCE B. BRAWER, *Associate Editor*

Number 58, Summer 1987

Paperback sourcebooks in
The Jossey-Bass Higher Education Series

Jossey-Bass Inc., Publishers
San Francisco • London

Charles R. Doty (ed.).
Developing Occupational Programs.
New Directions for Community Colleges, no. 58.
Volume XV, number 2.
San Francisco: Jossey-Bass, 1987.

New Directions for Community Colleges
Arthur M. Cohen, *Editor-in-Chief;* Florence B. Brawer, *Associate Editor*

New Directions for Community Colleges is published quarterly by Jossey-Bass Inc., Publishers (publication number USPS 121-710), in association with the ERIC Clearinghouse for Junior Colleges. *New Directions* is numbered sequentially—please order extra copies by sequential number. The volume and issue numbers above are included for the convenience of libraries. Second-class postage paid at San Francisco, California, and at additional mailing offices. POSTMASTER: Send address changes to Jossey-Bass, Inc., Publishers, 433 California Street, San Francisco, California 94104.

The material in this publication was prepared pursuant to a contract with the Office of Educational Research and Improvement, U.S. Department of Education. Contractors undertaking such projects under government sponsorship are encouraged to express freely their judgment in professional and technical matters. Prior to publication, the manuscript was submitted to the Center for the Study of Community Colleges for critical review and determination of professional competence. This publication has met such standards. Points of view or opinions, however, do not necessarily represent the official view or opinions of the Center for the Study of Community Colleges or the Office of Educational Research and Improvement.

Editorial correspondence should be sent to the Editor-in-Chief, Arthur M. Cohen, at the ERIC Clearinghouse for Junior Colleges, University of California, Los Angeles, California 90024.

Library of Congress Catalog Card Number LC 85-644753

International Standard Serial Number ISSN 0194-3081

International Standard Book Number ISBN 1-55542-959-9

Cover art by WILLI BAUM

Manufactured in the United States of America

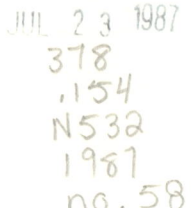

Office of Educational Research and Improvement U.S. Department of Education

Ordering Information

The paperback sourcebooks listed below are published quarterly and can be ordered either by subscription or single copy.

Subscriptions cost $52.00 per year for institutions, agencies, and libraries. Individuals can subscribe at the special rate of $39.00 per year *if payment is by personal check*. (Note that the full rate of $52.00 applies if payment is by institutional check, even if the subscription is designated for an individual.) Standing orders are accepted.

Single copies are available at $12.95 when payment accompanies order. (California, New Jersey, New York, and Washington, D.C., residents please include appropriate sales tax.) For billed orders, cost per copy is $12.95 plus postage and handling.

Substantial discounts are offered to organizations and individuals wishing to purchase bulk quantities of Jossey-Bass sourcebooks. Please inquire.

Please note that these prices are for the academic year 1986–1987 and are subject to change without notice. Also, some titles may be out of print and therefore not available for sale.

To ensure correct and prompt delivery, all orders must give either the *name of an individual* or an *official purchase order number*. Please submit your order as follows:

Subscriptions: specify series and year subscription is to begin.
Single Copies: specify sourcebook code (such as, CC1) and first two words of title.

Mail orders for United States and Possessions, Australia, New Zealand, Canada, Latin America, and Japan to:
Jossey-Bass Inc., Publishers
433 California Street
San Francisco, California 94104

Mail orders for all other parts of the world to:
Jossey-Bass Limited
28 Banner Street
London EC1Y 8QE

New Directions for Community Colleges Series
Arthur M. Cohen, *Editor-in-Chief*
Florence B. Brawer, *Associate Editor*

CC1 *Toward a Professional Faculty,* Arthur M. Cohen
CC2 *Meeting the Financial Crisis,* John Lombardi
CC3 *Understanding Diverse Students,* Dorothy M. Knoell

CC4   *Updating Occupational Education,* Norman C. Harris
CC5   *Implementing Innovative Instruction,* Roger H. Garrison
CC6   *Coordinating State Systems,* Edmund J. Gleazer, Jr., Roger Yarrington
CC7   *From Class to Mass Learning,* William M. Birenbaum
CC8   *Humanizing Student Services,* Clyde E. Blocker
CC9   *Using Instructional Technology,* George H. Voegel
CC10 *Reforming College Governance,* Richard C. Richardson, Jr.
CC11 *Adjusting to Collective Bargaining,* Richard J. Ernst
CC12 *Merging the Humanities,* Leslie Koltai
CC13 *Changing Managerial Perspectives,* Barry Heermann
CC14 *Reaching Out Through Community Service,* Hope M. Holcomb
CC15 *Enhancing Trustee Effectiveness,* Victoria Dziuba, William Meardy
CC16 *Easing the Transition from Schooling to Work,* Harry F. Silberman, Mark B. Ginsburg
CC17 *Changing Instructional Strategies,* James O. Hammons
CC18 *Assessing Student Academic and Social Progress,* Leonard L. Baird
CC19 *Developing Staff Potential,* Terry O'Banion
CC20 *Improving Relations with the Public,* Louis W. Bender, Benjamin R. Wygal
CC21 *Implementing Community-Based Education,* Ervin L. Harlacher, James F. Gollatscheck
CC22 *Coping with Reduced Resources,* Richard L. Alfred
CC23 *Balancing State and Local Control,* Searle F. Charles
CC24 *Responding to New Missions,* Myron A. Marty
CC25 *Shaping the Curriculum,* Arthur M. Cohen
CC26 *Advancing International Education,* Maxwell C. King, Robert L. Breuder
CC27 *Serving New Populations,* Patricia Ann Walsh
CC28 *Managing in a New Era,* Robert E. Lahti
CC29 *Serving Lifelong Learners,* Barry Heermann, Cheryl Coppeck Enders, Elizabeth Wine
CC30 *Using Part-Time Faculty Effectively,* Michael H. Parsons
CC31 *Teaching the Sciences,* Florence B. Brawer
CC32 *Questioning the Community College Role,* George B. Vaughan
CC33 *Occupational Education Today,* Kathleen F. Arns
CC34 *Women in Community Colleges,* Judith S. Eaton
CC35 *Improving Decision Making,* Mantha Mehallis
CC36 *Marketing the Program,* William A. Keim, Marybelle C. Keim
CC37 *Organization Development: Change Strategies,* James Hammons
CC38 *Institutional Impacts on Campus, Community, and Business Constituencies,* Richard L. Alfred
CC39 *Improving Articulation and Transfer Relationships,* Frederick C. Kintzer
CC40 *General Education in Two-Year Colleges,* B. Lamar Johnson
CC41 *Evaluating Faculty and Staff,* Al Smith
CC42 *Advancing the Liberal Arts,* Stanley F. Turesky
CC43 *Counseling: A Crucial Function for the 1980s,* Alice S. Thurston, William A. Robbins
CC44 *Strategic Management in the Community College,* Gunder A. Myran
CC45 *Designing Programs for Community Groups,* S. V. Martorana, William E. Piland
CC46 *Emerging Roles for Community College Leaders,* Richard L. Alfred, Paul A. Elsner, R. Jan LeCroy, Nancy Armes
CC47 *Microcomputer Applications in Administration and Instruction,* Donald A. Dellow, Lawrence H. Poole

CC48 *Customized Job Training for Business and Industry,* Robert J. Kopecek, Robert G. Clarke
CC49 *Ensuring Effective Governance,* William L. Deegan, James F. Gollattscheck
CC50 *Strengthening Financial Management,* Dale F. Campbell
CC51 *Active Trusteeship for a Changing Era,* Gary Frank Petty
CC52 *Maintaining Institutional Integrity,* Donald E. Puyear, George B. Vaughan
CC53 *Controversies and Decision Making in Difficult Economic Times,* Billie Wright Dziech
CC54 *The Community College and Its Critics,* L. Stephen Zwerling
CC55 *Advances in Instructional Technology,* George H. Voegel
CC56 *Applying Institutional Research,* John Losak
CC57 *Teaching the Developmental Education Student,* Kenneth M. Ahrendt

Contents

Editor's Notes 1
Charles R. Doty

1. **Federal Government Involvement in Technical Curriculum Development** 5
John G. Nealon
The federal government has long had a role in developing technical curricula for community colleges and technical institutes.

2. **The Challenge of Curriculum Development: From Idea to Reality** 9
Judith F. Raulf, Marilyn C. Ayres
This chapter provides a systematic development process to help in planning and implementing occupational programs that will prepare students to enter the marketplace.

3. **Needs Analysis: The Link to the Future** 25
Donald B. Smith
Data on changing labor market conditions are an important resource for those involved in curriculum development.

4. **Accrediting Occupational Programs** 35
Roland V. Stoodley, Jr.
Everyone on campus is affected by accreditation.

5. **What Teachers and Administrators Need to Know About Licensing and Certification Tests** 47
Charles J. Teryek
This chapter reviews the basic concepts of licensing and certification, noting their importance to the curriculum development process.

6. **Articulating Secondary and Postsecondary Occupational Programs** 57
Joseph P. Arnold
This chapter presents essential concepts, strategies, and recommendations for implementing vertical articulation between occupational programs at high schools and two-year colleges.

7. **General Education in the Occupational Curriculum: Why? To What Extent? With What Results?** 65
Dale F. Campbell, Mary T. Wood
Several colleges have taken innovative approaches to the problem of developing a general education component in the occupational curriculum.

8. Occupational Program Evaluation 77
Ted Martinez, Jr., Barbara S. Echord
This chapter presents a pragmatic approach to occupational program evaluation at different types of two-year institutions.

9. Sources and Information: Occupational Program Development 87
at the Postsecondary Level
Charles R. Doty, Mary P. Hardy
This chapter provides an annotated bibliography of ERIC materials.

Index 107

Editor's Notes

The goal of this sourcebook is to provide community college deans, chairs, and instructors with a conceptual framework for the process of occupational curriculum development. To achieve that goal, this volume examines the decision-making policies concerning curriculum development at the national, state, and local levels. The book also cites additional sources of information that may be consulted for further reading.

Why is there so much concern for occupational curriculum development? In 1981, Arns stated, "The problems associated with the move from an industrial society to a high-technological era are not yet comprehended" (p. vii). Today this statement is still true. Educators are trying to identify the factors that change the work force and to modify educational programs accordingly. This search for understanding was illustrated in the September 17, 1987, issue of the *Chronicle of Higher Education*. A heading on page one read, "Change in America"; the story included the following statement: "Between now and 2000, shifts in work and the work force are certain to transform much of U.S. higher education." The article also cited revealing statistics: 2 to 3 percent of the nation's work force (135 million) may need retraining by the year 2000; high-technology industries account for only 4 to 5 percent of the new positions created each year; and in the next ten years, six million more jobs are projected in executive, professional, and technical areas.

In addition to work-force changes, changes in the curricula at secondary schools are coming into play. New high school graduation requirements are forcing students away from applied arts curricula. This means that students will seek vocational and technical education after high school. (There could also be a large dropout rate from high school, but this is another potential problem.) The reduction of applied arts education will also mean that students will lack knowledge of tools, equipment, materials, and processes. The Harvard Committee (1945) recognized the consequences of reduced emphasis on the applied arts: "Such experience is important for the general education of all. Most students who expect to go to college are now offered an almost wholly verbal type of preparatory training, while hand training and the direct manipulation of objects are mainly reserved for the vocational fields. This is a serious mistake" (p. 175). Bronowski (1973) concurs: "The hand is the cutting edge of the mind. Civilization is not a collection of finished artifacts, it is the elaboration of processes. In the end, the march of man is the refinement of the hand in action" (p. 116).

Assuming that Bronowski is correct, this nation may be getting into trouble if education deemphasizes hands-on learning. Today's economy has been described as an information-disseminating economy, but anyone with any sense knows that knowledge is gained by problem-solving, using tools, equipment, materials, and processes; these are the ingredients of manufacturing, and manufacturing is the foundation of our nation's power and influence (Schuman, 1986).

Thus, there are important reasons to study occupational curriculum development: People must be prepared for changes in the workplace, and postsecondary occupational education can help workers adjust to those changes. What is more fundamental, knowledge of tools, equipment, materials, and processes is vital to the education of every person, is essential to the progress of civilization, and is the basis from which knowledge is derived.

The chapters in this volume address several important aspects of the curriculum-development process. In Chapter One, John G. Nealon examines the critical role of decision making at the national level and the effects of the federal role on community colleges and technical institutes. I believe that Nealon's suggestion for increased collaboration between education and industry is essential, but I also believe that occupational educators should strive for changes in national policies that affect technical curricula.

In Chapter Two, Judith F. Raulf and Marilyn C. Ayres describe a theoretical model for curriculum development and provide a flowchart illustrating the steps in developing and securing approval for a new occupational program. Then, because data collection and analysis are so important, Donald B. Smith, in Chapter Three, gives a thorough listing of resources to be consulted in finding data on the changing labor market.

Accreditation, addressed in Chapter Four by Roland V. Stoodley, Jr., is one of the key indicators of professionalism. Casey (1986) states, "There is no question in my mind that any agency that goes through the accreditation process has to improve its efficiency, service to the public and esprit de corps" (p. 49). Stoodley provides a clear description of this process.

Licensing and certification tests have become crucial to a person's being allowed to work in almost every occupation. In Chapter Five, Charles J. Teryek explains the basics (terminology, legality, student preparation) of such tests. Ignoring such testing could result in the elimination of occupational programs.

Vertical articulation between secondary vocational programs and postsecondary institutions is one of the major changes in education today. Joseph P. Arnold describes the basic principles of such articulation in Chapter Six.

General education, the type of education we want each student to experience, is especially crucial in a changing society. In Chapter Seven,

Dale F. Campbell and Mary T. Wood provide a succinct analysis of questions concerning the degree to which general education should be incorporated into technical curricula and the ways in which colleges have performed this task.

Because no one wants to be criticized, program evaluation is often ignored or poorly conducted. In Chapter Eight, Ted Martinez, Jr., and Barbara S. Echord describe a community college program evaluation system that works.

Chapter Nine provides an annotated bibliography of further resources in the ERIC data base.

Charles R. Doty
Editor

References

Arns, K. F. (ed.). *Occupational Education Today.* New Directions for Community Colleges, no. 33. San Francisco: Jossey-Bass, 1981.
Bronowski, J. *The Ascent of Man.* Boston: Little, Brown, 1973.
Casey, K. "Four Jersey Police Departments Seek Accreditation." Newark, N.J.: *The Sunday Star Ledger,* Oct. 19, 1986, Sec. 1, p. 49.
"Change in America." *Chronicle of Higher Education,* Sept. 17, 1986, p. 1.
Harvard Committee. *General Education in a Free Society.* Cambridge, Mass.: Harvard University Press, 1945.
Schuman, C. C. "Vocational Educators' Response to a Perceived Educational Crisis." Presentation to the Northeast Regional State Councils on Vocational Education, Atlantic City, N.J., Sept. 26, 1986.

Charles R. Doty is the adviser in technical education at the Graduate School of Education of the State University of New Jersey, Rutgers.

The federal government has long had a role in developing technical curricula for community colleges and technical institutes.

Federal Government Involvement in Technical Curriculum Development

John G. Nealon

Prior to the 1950s, the federal government played no significant role in the development of curriculum materials. By the late 1950s, however, changing perceptions of the practical value of academic education, coupled with concerns about national security and the country's critical need for trained scientists, engineers, and technicians, led to increasing government involvement in curriculum development for vocational and technical education (Atkin and House, 1981). The federal government's role in vocational curriculum development was authorized and encouraged by Congress in the Vocational Education Act of 1963 and its subsequent amendments. Congress reaffirmed its position by requiring curriculum development under Title IV of the Carl D. Perkins Vocational Act in 1984.

This chapter reviews the outcomes of the curriculum development activities of the United States Department of Education, with particular focus on the curriculum materials that have been made available, and offers support for a continued government role in this area.

A Review of the Projects

In 1965, the Technical Education Research Center (TERC) was created to develop curricula in new and emerging technologies of national importance. Conceived by eight presidents of two-year postsecondary institutions, TERC's focus was on serving the curricular needs of two-year technical education. In the late 1960s and the early 1970s, TERC received four federal grants for the design and development of curricula in the following areas: laser/electro-optics technology, electromechanical technology, nuclear medicine, and biomedical equipment.

The laser/electro-optics technology (LEOT) project was representative in size and format of all four TERC projects (Hull, 1975). Funded at a level of $1 million over a four-year period, the project resulted in the development and field testing of a curriculum planning guide and 101 instructional modules designed to prepare technicans for employment. The content of the modules, which were prepared by technical experts working in the LEOT field, was based on an analysis of the duties and tasks of the LEO technician as they had been identified by a national advisory committee. The instructional philosophy adopted in the materials emphasized laboratory learning, that is, the learning of theoretical principles by hands-on practice. Each of the modules contained an introduction describing the rationale for the unit; student performance objectives; theoretical background; lists of needed equipment and materials; experiment and problems sections; and references for supplemental reading and writing. The modules were grouped into learning units, which were further grouped into ten courses.

Between 1974 and 1977, more than 50,000 educational units were distributed to more than thirty-five institutions. TERC's dissemination model involved no- or low-cost publicity, the targeting of areas of high-LEOT employment potential, the organization of state and regional meetings for representatives of interested institutions and employers, and the consensual selection of training sites (Hull, 1978).

Between 1974 and 1978, TERC received more than $1.65 million in contracts to develop curriculum guides, and 359 instructional modules for the training of nuclear reactor (plant) operators, radiation protection technicians, nuclear quality assurance and quality control technicians, nuclear materials processing technicians, nuclear instrumentation and control technicians, and energy conservation technicians. In addition, TERC received two grants for the development of a program entitled "Unified Technical Concepts in Physics," which yielded thirteen "concept" modules and 177 "applications" modules.

In 1980, the Southern Division of TERC became the Center for Occupational Research and Development (CORD). With federal support, CORD has developed 50 instructional modules for job safety and health and conducted needs and task analyses for the fields of robotics and manufacturing. While CORD continues to develop curricula in emerging fields, its primary sources of financial support are private industry and educational consortia. For example, the Electrical Utilities Technical Education Council, representing twenty-two electrical utilities, provided $1 million to CORD for the development of training modules for power plant personnel, while a consortium of forty-one states and provinces has supported the development of a high school vocational course in applied physics.

Current Policy and Practice

Approximately five years ago, with the advent of the Reagan administration, the Department of Education promulgated a general internal policy that no national curricula would be imposed on the country. The policy, which was intended to protect academic freedom and forestall the development of elementary and secondary curricula with affective and attitudinal content, also had the unfortunate effect of ceasing curriculum development in postsecondary technical occupational education.

Other branches of the federal government continue to support the development of curricula for national dissemination. These agencies include the Environmental Protection Agency, the Department of Health and Human Services' Administration on Aging and Children's Bureau, the National Institutes of Health, the National Oceanic and Atmospheric Administration's National Sea Grants Program, and the U.S. armed forces. TERC itself is currently focusing on computer applications to education in science and mathematics, with support from the National Science Foundation and other sources.

The efforts of these agencies notwithstanding, it is unlikely that curriculum development will be funded on a broad scale by the national government. While Title IV of P.L. 98-524 mandates the development of curricula, discretionary funds for such items as the National Center for Research in Vocational Education and the National Occupational Information Coordinating Council are limited and not likely to be expanded.

The implications of these policy and financial constraints are especially detrimental for high-technology occupations. Even though projections indicate that no more than 10 to 15 percent of the nation's work force will be involved in high technology, these occupations are vital to the survival of the national economy. The development of professionally designed curricula to train workers in these fields is likely to be beyond the financial resources of any one institution or state. Financial support for the development of curriculum materials and for provision of training equipment and facilities will of necessity come from educational institutions and the private sector.

Future Relationships

It is always a hazardous undertaking when two primary social institutions must, for the good of both, engage in what amounts to a shotgun marriage. In the case of curriculum development, there seem to be few alternatives to cooperative efforts involving the private industrial sector and the public educational sector. Both must work together to provide meaningful education for students and to keep each other honest. Left to its own devices, the private sector, which generally considers education to be an overhead expense, would narrowly educate people in the specific technical areas that best serve business interests, thus limiting technicians' potential for lateral mobility in their work. Postsecondary institutions in turn lack the capital, equipment, and facilities of the private sector. Unable to provide students with adequate hands-on experience, colleges could be tempted to provide theoretically broad education that would lack the precision needed by industry.

The education of modern technicians is complicated and will require a symbiotic relationship between business and education to support a high-technology economy.

References

Atkin, J. M., and House, E. R. "The Federal Role in Curriculum Development, 1950-1980." *Educational Evaluation and Policy Analysis*, 1981, *3* (5), 5-36.

Hull, D. M. *Development of Generalizable Educational Programs in Laser/Electro-Optics Technology: Final Report.* Waco, Tex.: Technical Education Research Center, 1975. (ED 112 433)

Hull, D. M. *A Dissemination Model for New Technical Education Programs. Final Report.* Waco, Tex.: Technical Education Research Center, 1978. (ED 166 431)

John G. Nealon is chief of the Special Programs Branch, Office of Vocational and Adult Education, United States Department of Education. This chapter was written by Mr. Nealon as a private citizen. No official support from or endorsement by the Department of Education should be inferred.

This chapter provides a systematic development process to help in planning and implementing occupational programs that will prepare students to enter the marketplace.

The Challenge of Curriculum Development: From Idea to Reality

Judith F. Raulf, Marilyn C. Ayres

Historically, postsecondary educational institutions have responded to the training needs of business and industry. Rapid changes in technology, however, have created problems in keeping programs up-to-date and in initiating new programs. The basic question that educators in community colleges and technical institutes must answer concerning change is "How can we be sure to meet the needs of business and industry and at the same time develop programs that meet the needs of the federal government, the community, and the individual?" Grubb (1984, p. 429) concurs with the idea that the proposing institution should be cautious not to develop occupational programs that, for the most part, "serve only the interests of business and industry and ultimately weaken the education mission of the community college."

To answer and solve these questions and problems properly, educators must search for programs that have a future for students and institutions. This search must be conducted in a thorough and systematic manner. Using the requirements for the state of New Jersey as an example, we shall present an approach for planning, developing, approving, and evaluating occupational curricula.

Figure 1 presents the phases of program identification, program documentation, and program execution. Phase 1 addresses the advisory committee, the feasibility study, institutional capability, and articulation with educational institutions and with business and industry.

Figure 2 is a flowchart of phase 1. Phase 2 of Figure 1 presents the procedures involved in developing a preliminary program announcement, a program approval document, and the state evaluation of these program materials—all key components of the occupational curriculum approval process. These procedures are shown in another flowchart, Figure 3. Phase 3 of Figure 1 takes the program developer through implementation and evaluation of the program and of any enhancements required for program improvement. Phase 3 is elaborated in Figure 4. These flowcharts will help planners meet the challenge of taking curriculum development from idea to reality. Economics, technology, and demand will have an impact on the whole process.

For beginning the identification process in phase 1, leaders in business and industry provide unmatched expertise. The formulation of an advisory committee, which is composed of these leaders, is pivotal to the proposed program.

Phase 1: Program Identification

Advisory Committees. The federal Vocational Education Act of 1976 requires agencies and programs that receive federal vocational education funds to establish local councils that will provide advice on topics such as current job needs, skill requirements, relevancy of courses and programs, and state-of-the-art equipment. The act suggests that advisory councils include members from the general public, especially from business, industry, and labor. Federal Public Law 98-524, Oct. 19, 1984, does not specifically require local advisory occupational councils, but councils are required at the state and national levels. Holcomb, Morris, and Callahan (1977) suggest that committee membership include faculty, employers, employment agencies, and representatives from various special groups.

It is important to note that the committees are advisory bodies that provide advice and counsel. Six to ten members make a manageable group, provided that each of the members is able and willing to work with the others. The federal Vocational Education Act stipulates that the committee meet at least once each year. The proposing institution may want to meet formally once each semester. There could also be ongoing informal contact with individual members of the committee who have expertise in particular areas.

Anderson (1983) recognized that local advisory committees provide the necessary link between local business and industry and postsecondary educational institutions, a link that is of paramount importance for keep-

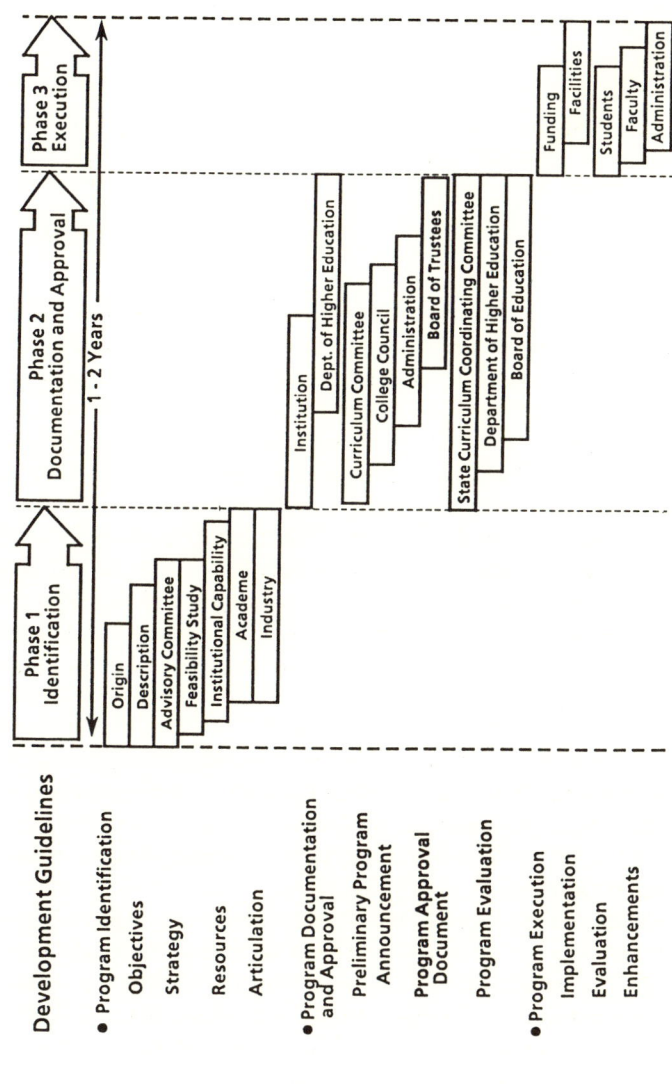

Figure 1. Curriculum Development Overview

Figure 2. Program Approval Process: Phase 1

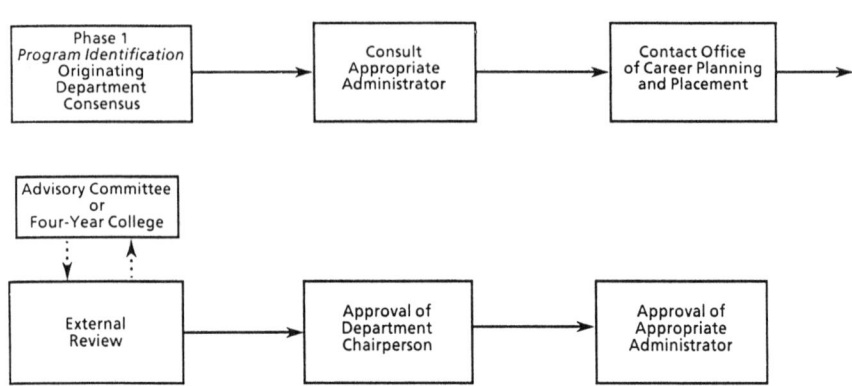

ing occupational curricula and training programs up to date. Advisory committees are vital to the development of high-quality educational programs. Individual members bring a wealth of experience and expertise in their fields of specialization. They can be trainers in cooperative education; excellent student recruiters; helpers in graduate placement; skilled public relations people; and helpers in instructor recruitment and selection, development of curriculum materials, and program evaluation.

A handbook from Hagerstown Junior College in Maryland (1982) presents the primary functions of an advisory committee: (1) to provide advice about development, maintenance, operation, and modification of occupational programs, (2) to suggest types of educational and technical services needed by the community, and (3) to participate in program evaluation.

Grubb (1984, p. 432) pointed out that advisory committee links or partnerships "are both the means of securing hardware and instructors in rapidly developing high-tech fields and the way of providing specific training for . . . new and expanding companies." As mentioned earlier, advisory-committee selection may occur at the same time that the feasibility study is being conducted.

Feasibility Study. A proposed occupational program may appear viable to those who are developing it, but sufficient data are necessary to support the program for final approval by the college's or technical school's administration and by the relevant state department. A feasibility study is required for approval and implementation of the program.

A number of sources should be consulted in gathering national, state, and local data to support the hypothesis that a particular program should be offered. Holcomb, Morris, and Callahan (1977) suggest that the proposing institution tap the resources of governmental agencies, licensing and accreditation agencies, business and industry, and other educational

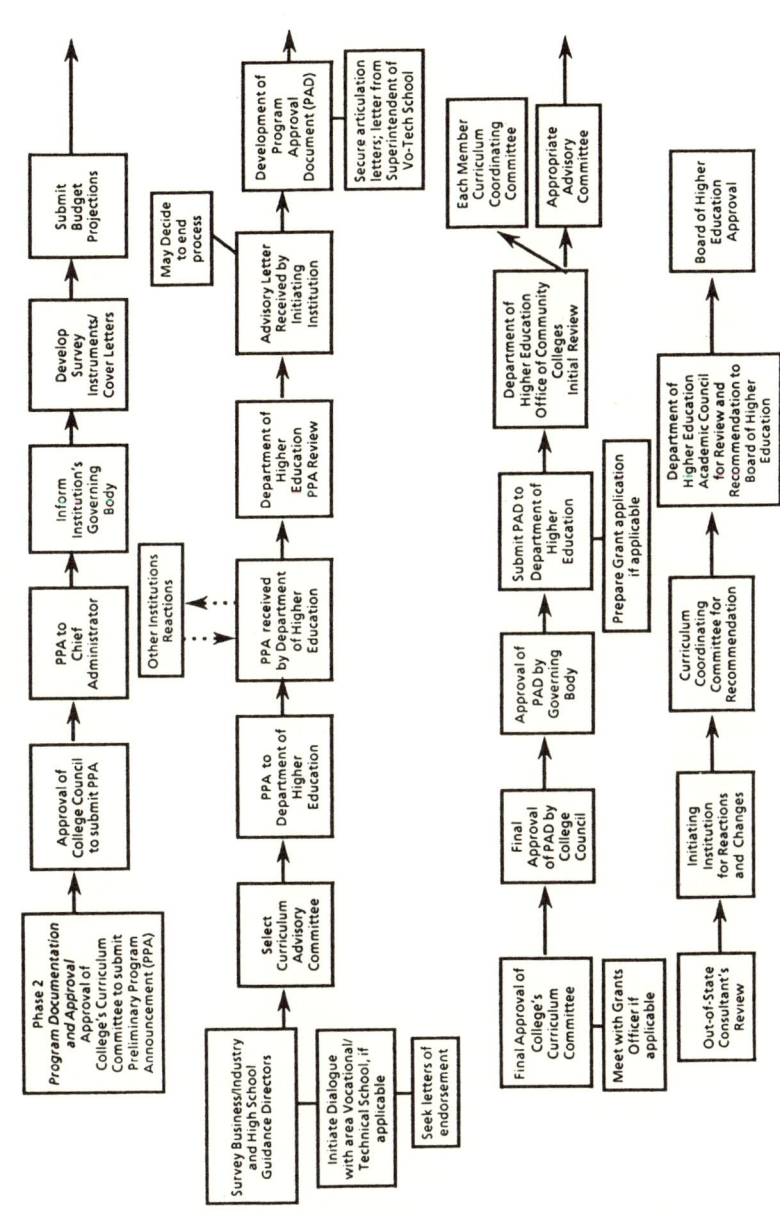

Figure 3. Program Approval Process: Phase 2

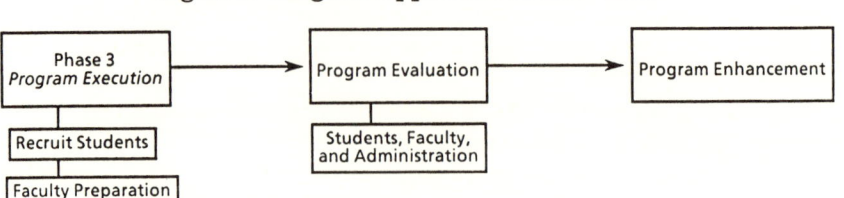

Figure 4. Program Approval Process: Phase 3

```
┌─────────────────┐      ┌─────────────────┐      ┌─────────────────┐
│    Phase 3      │─────▶│Program Evaluation│─────▶│Program Enhancement│
│Program Execution│      └─────────────────┘      └─────────────────┘
└─────────────────┘              │
        │                ┌─────────────────┐
┌─────────────────┐      │Students, Faculty,│
│ Recruit Students│      │and Administration│
└─────────────────┘      └─────────────────┘
        │
┌─────────────────┐
│Faculty Preparation│
└─────────────────┘
```

institutions in the area. The proposing institution's own office of career planning and placement can supply national and state data from such sources as the *Occupational Outlook Handbook*, the *Dictionary of Occupational Titles*, and selected professional publications. Publications from state departments or bureaus of labor statistics will also provide state or regional data.

If the proposing institution's office of career planning and placement has access to data bases concerning national and state statistics on job projections, the developers of the proposed program may wish to include those data in the document. A word of caution is appropriate. The proposing institution should be aware that sometimes state or regional data do not accurately reflect the proposing institution's marketplace or service area; instead, they may reflect a statewide or regional base.

For these reasons, it is important that the proposing institution clearly present local data to support the need for the program. How can this task be accomplished? A survey can elicit information from business and industry that will give an accurate picture of occupations as they may be related to the proposed program. Decision makers need data to support the proposing institution's theory that sufficient career opportunities will be available in the surrounding area to justify a full program.

The data from the survey of demand in the local service area should include:
1. Number of local agencies, businesses, and industries relevant to program graduates that were contacted
2. Number of respondents
3. Number of persons now employed in the types of positions for which the program will train students
4. Number of persons hired in these positions in the previous year
5. Number of projected positions
6. Willingness of employers to hire the program's graduates
7. Rate of turnover and estimate of increased need
8. Types of positions and yearly salary ranges available to program graduates.

Some sense of student interest must be part of the data. A survey of high school guidance departments should be developed and administered. A survey instrument of ten or fewer short-response questions is suggested. Some sample questions are:
1. Do graduates of your school pursue postsecondary education or training in [name of proposed program]?
2. Please indicate the number of your graduates who have enrolled in postsecondary education in [name of proposed program] for the last three years, as well as an estimate for next year.
3. Please list the educational institutions in which these graduates have enrolled.
4. Do you offer any courses in [name of proposed program]?

The proposing institution should not overlook contributions from the members of the curriculum advisory committee. Valuable data can be obtained from members who are concerned about the quality of education of their future employees and who wish to help the proposing institution use its resources wisely.

Letters of endorsement for the program will become part of the proposing institution's final document. Members of the advisory committee, selected respondents to the survey of business and industry, and high school guidance directors are people from whom such letters can be solicited.

Holcomb, Morris, and Callahan (1977) cited the use of data from institutions that have similar programs as an aid to the proposing institution in projecting enrollment and retention. They also pointed out that job information data must focus on the nature of job opportunities, titles, skills, knowledge, and attitudes for placement.

Some decision makers may feel the need to justify implementing a new occupational program solely on the basis of statistics on available jobs. Timing is crucial. If a proposing institution gathers its local data too early, they may be insufficient to ensure approval of the program.

The recommendations of the advisory committee and the results of the feasibility study will lead educators to determine institutional capability, the next step in the development process. Zenger and Zenger's (1982) ten-step process suggests that at this stage the elements to be considered include facilities, equipment, materials, budget, and personnel.

Institutional Capability. The institution's proposal to offer an adequate new program must include a commitment to faculty, facilities, library holdings, laboratories, support services, and operating budget. Funding of up-to-date equipment and facilities is a frequent problem, especially in high-technology programs.

Posner and others (1975) cited a number of concerns in what they termed the "support" area: personnel qualifications, class size, faculty-student ratio, time, initial capital investment, support services, personnel costs, remedial services, and clerical costs. When reviewing these economic factors, the proposing institution must stop and seriously ask if it has the necessary qualified instructional staff; buildings and space, equipment, and materials; counseling, placement, financial aid, and clerical support; library holdings, staff, and services; and federal, state, regional, local, and private foundation funds. If the answer is yes, then the proposing institution may proceed with its investigation of articulation with business and educational institutions.

Articulation. There are two kinds of articulation: with business and industry, and with educational institutions, including high schools and four-year colleges. Articulation with business and industry provides information exchange, and articulation with high schools and four-year colleges can aid recruitment.

Community colleges and technical institutes can establish themselves as information links between research and engineering divisions of large businesses and industries and other potential employers in the local area. The proposing institution can provide information about an emerging occupation through seminars, workshops, and consulting services. In turn, business and industry can provide members for the program's advisory committee who are experts in their fields; hardware; software; curriculum materials; and, more important, prospective students from among their employees who need training or retraining in specific areas.

Vertical articulation with local secondary and vocational-technical schools, and with four-year schools to which the program's graduates transfer, is important. Vincent (1986) states, "In the years ahead, community colleges will remain a wellspring for all of higher education, if they are given both the means to carry out their missions and the cooperation with senior colleges and universities they need to become full partners in assuring access throughout academe for students of ability" (p. 92). In an age of declining enrollment, duplication of programs must be avoided, and articulation becomes more important than in times of high enrollment. Proliferation of programs when enrollments are low could force some institutions prematurely to discontinue their high-cost programs.

Program graduates need assurances that they can transfer to four-year colleges without substantial loss of credit. Appropriate written articulation agreements should be made between the proposing institution and four-year colleges to ensure that the program's graduates can transfer to four-year colleges and have junior-year status. Articulation agreements with vocational-technical schools and with local high schools can help ensure their graduates advanced placement. Several successful 2 + 2 programs have been implemented in recent years because of scarce resources and declining enrollment.

Institutions close to one another may want to consider proposing joint programs with vocational-technical schools or with other colleges and technical institutes to share laboratory facilities, library holdings, and faculty. Students may be willing to travel a reasonable distance if they know that challenging, high-quality education is available at nearby schools.

Once the proposing institution has weighed all the data and the decision to implement a new program has been made, phase 2 of the curriculum development overview begins.

Phase 2: Program Documentation and Approval

Preliminary Program Announcement. In New Jersey, a preliminary program announcement must be prepared, approved, and submitted to the state department of higher education. The preliminary program announcement acquaints all higher education institutions in the state with new programs being considered by other institutions and permits the state department of higher education to react to program proposals early in their development. The state department's reactions to program proposals at this stage are only advisory. The submission of a preliminary program announcement to the state department of higher education does not commit an institution to proceed with the complete process. The preliminary program announcement should include the following:

1. Name of the proposing institution and date
2. Name of the proposed program
3. Objectives of the program
4. Relationship of the program to institutional and state master plans
5. Names of similar programs in the state, and a description of how this program differs from those already offered
6. Assessment of the need for the program, including preliminary evidence of student interest and labor market need
7. Projected enrollments for the first and fifth years
8. Date program is to be offered
9. Description of efforts to ensure adequate articulation with other programs in the state.

Feldman (1977, p. 8) called this the estimation process. She cited four main areas that should be addressed: identity, articulation, resources, and employment-transfer. Feldman suggested that in the initial stages of the process, these questions be addressed: What is the proposed content of the new program? Where does the program fit in terms of master planning, regional planning, and individual campus career thrust? What is the career field of the program? In general, what new resources are needed? What are the identified manpower needs? Is the program transferable?

The preliminary program announcement is presented to the institution's curriculum committee and college council for a recommendation on whether to proceed with the development of a program approval document. The curriculum committee includes faculty, administrators, and students who represent a cross-section of the college community. The college council is an advisory body to the president and is composed of department chairpersons, standing committee chairpersons, deans, elected faculty, and student representatives.

In New Jersey, the preliminary program announcement must be submitted to the state department of higher education at least one year before the program's implementation. The state department of higher education reviews the preliminary program announcement for clarity and completeness. It then disseminates copies to all the state's colleges for their comments, which are limited to the proposed program's impact on the other institutions in such areas as duplication, student pool, and articulation.

Once the state department of higher education receives the comments, it sends the proposing institution an advisory letter that outlines the comments received, suggests factors to be considered in developing the new program, and either encourages or discourages further efforts to develop the new program. The state department at this stage will raise as many of its concerns about the proposed program as possible. The proposing institution may decide to end the process after reviewing the advisory letter. If the institution elects to continue the process, it must prepare a program approval document.

Program Approval Document. The program approval document presents complete information on the proposed program in concise form. This is the information that determines final approval of the program. The final document will be reviewed by decision makers at the proposing institution and at the state level; therefore, the program approval document should express its ideas, methodology, and goals in a way that is accurate, clear, and logical. The document should be written so that anyone can read and understand it completely, without recourse to other people, books, or data. No questions or issues should be raised that are not answered. The document's format, organization, content, and supportive data will be evaluated by the state department of higher education.

It is important to show why the proposed program was chosen over other programs, given particular institutional interests and priorities. The program approval document will require detailed cost factors—personnel, equipment, and operating expenses. Descriptions of the kinds of equipment as well as the extent to which it will be used should be given. Feldman (1977) suggests including descriptions of the required space and equipment and considering grants to underwrite start-up costs.

The program approval document must discuss articulation and transfer. Letters of articulation from senior institutions to which program graduates transfer would be appropriate to include. A letter from the superintendent of a vocational-technical school, indicating that he or she was consulted in the development of the proposed program, might also become part of the approval document.

Institutional Approval. Before the program approval document can be submitted to the state department of higher education, approvals from within the proposing institution will be required. After the proposed program has been through an exhaustive study at the departmental level, it is ready for a second presentation to the college curriculum committee.

It should be noted that the administration has been involved in the early stages of the proposal process. The individuals proposing the program need the support of the division dean for later advice and counsel. In addition, the division dean can authorize release time for program study and development. The division dean keeps the academic dean informed of the status of the proposed program.

Although the curriculum committee by now has given initial authorization for the development of the program approval document, at this point the committee evaluates the proposed program for its viability as one of the institution's full-fledged degree or certificate offerings. The following information should be presented to the curriculum committee for evaluation:
1. Feasibility study data
2. Advisory committee input
3. Supply-and-demand data from needs assessment
4. Student interest data from survey
5. Budget considerations for faculty, space, laboratories, support staff, and equipment
6. Curriculum or program of study
7. Course descriptions for catalogue.

The presentation is then made to the college council. The recommendation for action on the program by the college council is submitted to the president. If the recommendation is affirmative and is accepted by the president, the final group of endorsers at the institution is the board of trustees or other governing body. The proposed program is now ready for presentation in its final form to the state department of higher education. Educators must assume that when the proposed program is submitted to the department of higher education, no modifications will be made by the proposing institution.

Department of Higher Education Review. This review of the program approval document involves the staff of the state office of community colleges, the department of higher education, the curriculum coordinating committee, advisory committees, and out-of-state consultants. In New Jersey, program approval documents must be submitted at least nine months before a program is recommended for implementation. Multiple copies are sent to the state department of higher education by the president of the institution.

During this evaluation process, the department of higher education uses out-of-state consultants to review program approval documents. The consultant and a representative from the state department of higher education visit the institution and meet with the faculty member who developed the document and with other administrators before preparing a report. The consultant's report, together with comments from other evaluators, is forwarded to the institution. On the strength of the comments, the institution may or may not revise the program approval document. Again, multiple copies, complete with revisions, are submitted with the document in final form.

The state then schedules the proposed program on the agenda of its curriculum coordinating committee and circulates copies of the program approval document to the committee members. The curriculum coordinating committee is made up of deans, trustees, presidents of New Jersey colleges and universities, and a liaison from the state office of community colleges. Usually representatives from the proposing institution attend the curriculum coordinating committee meeting to present the program and answer questions. The committee will either approve the program, request revisions, or reject it. If the proposed program is approved, the department of higher education will inform the institution when the program will be considered for its next review by the state board of higher education.

The department of higher education requires the following items to be included in the appendix of the program approval document:
1. Course list, including credits and contact hours
2. Course descriptions for specialized offerings
3. Evaluation criteria for program
4. Personnel requirements
5. Feasibility study on manpower demand for program
6. Letters of endorsement.

Phase 3, inauguration of the program at the institution, begins once the proposed program is approved by the state board of higher education. The program is now in the early stages of its realization.

Phase 3: Program Execution

The implementation of the approved program will require marketing, with emphasis placed on groups that showed the most interest in the program during the feasibility study. Several students may already be taking general education courses as they wait for the new program. If a program begins in the fall, publicity should appear in the preceding semester's tabloid. (No program in New Jersey, however, can be scheduled and publicized before final state approval.)

When the institutional budget is submitted, matching funds for vocational education grants might be considered. An educator must be ready to write a grant proposal if funds are available. Such funding is more readily available for new programs than for existing programs, especially in the technologies. Therefore, if the program is approved and grant proposals are submitted in the spring before implementation, equipment will be in place and operational by the second semester of the new program. Planning is required when funding will depend on grants.

Find the best educators available for the new program. If new faculty are required, the recruitment process will take place during the preceding semester. If current faculty will have a role in the new program, adequate lead time for class preparation will be necessary. Schroeder and Furtado (1986, p. 36) suggest that those experienced educators will have to prepare themselves for new technologies to the point of "being comfortable about feeling uncomfortable." Anyone preparing a staff development program to upgrade technical competence should examine the report by Doty (1985).

Equipment sharing among departments or institutions may be possible. This opportunity will provide smoother implementation for the first several semesters. Sharing resources provides the faculty with time to recruit students and refine course offerings. New equipment can be added gradually as the program becomes established. If new equipment will be purchased, selection must be made carefully, with concern for the useful life of the equipment.

Course descriptions have already been prepared for the program approval document approved by the state. However, textbooks, behavioral objectives, and syllabi must also be chosen during implementation. Again, high-quality education begins with strong faculty and careful preparation. Implementation is the time to establish a high-quality program.

Program Evaluation

Program quality and content relevance are two key factors to assess in the evaluation of a new occupational curriculum. The need for continual updating of curricula is critical. Several groups and phases should be involved in the process.

Curriculum Committee. Input from the institution's curriculum committee is vital. The curriculum committee should be a standing committee of the institution. Just as it was used to develop the occupational program, so should it be used to evaluate it. After two years, the curriculum committee should examine the program in terms of meeting program objectives. Thereafter the committee should review it on a five-year cycle.

Course Evaluation. Academic course evaluation must be done yearly to ensure the relevance of the course. Each academic department of the institution should be required to evaluate the courses in its curriculum. Committees of departmental faculty should review course syllabi, objectives, and teaching methodology.

Student Course Evaluation. The students are the consumers of our programs; their input must not be taken lightly. Each semester, students should be asked to complete surveys that seek their opinions about course content, delivery systems, and relevance.

Program Advisory Committee. The expertise of this group was helpful in the developmental stages of the program, and it can also aid evaluation. The committee is composed of professionals in the field who can provide valuable information about current job requirements and new techniques. Members of the committee can also provide follow-up information about the skills of program graduates.

Outside Accrediting Agencies. National accrediting agencies conduct periodic accreditation reviews that aid immeasurably in program evaluation. Extensive self-study reports that are required by the accrediting agency can form the basis for program evaluation.

Faculty. Faculty members are alert and responsive to necessary program modifications and course revisions. Their attendance at professional conferences and continuing education courses helps them remain on the cutting edge of innovative programs.

Summary

As educators, our greatest challenge is developing new programs that produce rewarding career opportunities in ever-changing occupational environments. Perhaps the traditional approaches for planning, developing, approving, implementing, and evaluating occupational curricula, as presented here, seem too complex. State departments of education, boards of regents, and other approval bodies must streamline their procedures, rules, and regulations to allow proposing institutions to implement viable occupational curricula in a timely fashion. This will be crucial to high-technology programs if educators are to keep promises in the right place, at the right time.

References

Anderson, W. *Vocational Education Advisory Committees.* Sacramento, Calif.: California Community Colleges, 1983. (ED 233 769)

Doty, C. R. *Technical Upgrading.* New Brunswick, N.J.: Department of Vocational and Technical Education, Rutgers University, 1985. (ED 262 829)

Feldman, B. "Procedure for New Course Development." Practicum presented to Nova University, 1977. (ED 133 007)

Grubb, W. "The Bandwagon Once More: Vocational Preparation for High-Tech Occupations." *Harvard Educational Review,* 1984, *54* (4), 429–451.

Hagerstown Junior College. *Hagerstown Junior College Advisory Committee Handbook.* Hagerstown, Md.: Hagerstown Junior College, 1982. (ED 215 746)

Holcomb, R., Morris, W., and Callahan, W. V. *Guidelines for Occupational Program Planning: A Handbook.* Los Angeles: Los Angeles Community College District, 1977. (ED 143 404)

Posner, G., Egner, J. R., Hedlund, D., Young, R., Chickering-Clay, L., Deay, A., and Koffel, K. *Program Planning in Two-Year Colleges: A Handbook.* Ithaca, New York: Cornell Institute for Research and Development in Occupational Education, State University of New York, 1975. (ED 112 957)

Schroeder, B., and Furtado, L. "Curriculum Improvement." *Business Education Forum,* 1986, *40* (8), 32–40.

Vincent, W. "How We Can Make Sure That Community Colleges Remain a Wellspring for All of Higher Education?" *The Chronicle of Higher Education,* April 16, 1986, p. 92.

Zenger, W., and Zenger, S. *Curriculum Planning: A Ten-Step Process.* Palo Alto, Calif.: R & E Research Associates, 1982. (ED 227 562)

Judith F. Raulf is assistant dean of the Division of Academic Affairs at County College of Morris in Randolph, New Jersey. She has served as chairperson of the college's curriculum committee for two years, developing curricula in office studies, agriculture, and media.

Marilyn C. Ayres is chair of the Department of Office Systems at County College of Morris in Randolph, N.J. She has served as chairperson of the college's curriculum committee and has been involved in the development of curricula in office studies and telecommunications.

As traditional two-year colleges move from the role of junior colleges, becoming full-service community colleges, a better understanding of the resources available to conduct program needs analysis has become critical.

Needs Analysis: The Link to the Future

Donald B. Smith

So often one encounters academic deans and vice-presidents who sense the need for a program, take only the time to develop the paperwork for some state agency, and complain because they really do not grasp the proposed program. Asked if they are aware of statistical projections, they usually respond negatively to the use of such figures. Asked if the proposed program follows evolving trends, they may give positive responses, but they do not want to be asked about these trends. Ask if the proposed program identifies with economic projections, emerging occupational categories, or evolving industries, and you are apt to receive a defensive response.

In fact, an expensive program often is defended on the basis of a select group of individuals who have given their valuable time graciously and honorably to advisory meetings, which are orchestrated by those whose vested interests are best served by soliciting statements supportive of the program in question, so that curriculum developers can get on with the paperwork and coordinators can tell all who will listen how they are bringing the latest in high-technology programs to the community. The key word here is *select*, which suggests the exclusion of those who might contribute negative or alternative information to the discussion. In the end, one may have a parochial program that may indeed serve an immediate job market but may not be able to sustain itself because of saturation or a changing job market.

There is no substitute for hard work. This hard work can be categorized into several "must do" steps if one is truly going to have a grasp of where the jobs are going to be. Seven major topical areas can be identified:

- How federal, state, and local unemployment figures can help one understand the overview of actual and evolving trends
- Sources of federal, state, and local employment projections and their use in understanding the directions the world of work is taking, for which new training programs might be needed
- The use of periodicals, newspapers, and government publications to provide an understanding of economic projections that will affect existing local and emerging industries
- Sources of emerging occupational categories, as identified by industrial associations, forecasting industries, and forecasting authors
- The projections for new industries, if any, by state and local economic agencies
- Sources of local manufacturers and service industries that can be used for industrial surveys
- The use of advisory committees from areas identified by the above research and resources.

Each may be developed into individual concepts and exercises, and all can come together to give the directions needed to begin the development of a new program.

Federal, State, and Local Unemployment Figures

This author has found valuable information in both national and state unemployment figures. During the 1981-1982 recession's low point, one heard unemployment figures daily. Community and technical colleges received encouragement to "put America back to work." The catch to achieving this became apparent only to those who truly studied the unemployment figures. While we were being told of the national unemployment average of 11.4 percent for all Americans, a closer look showed a 16.9 percent rate of unemployment for Hispanics and 21.7 percent for blacks. Month after month, this imbalance contrasted with today's "recovery," showing an unemployment rate of 7.0 percent for the total civilian population, compared with 10.8 percent for Hispanics and 15.1 percent for blacks. This author has found it very beneficial to graph these rates as a quick and ready reference for unemployment. National figures are available in the *Monthly Labor Review, Employment and Earnings,* and *News*. All of these are monthly publications of the U.S. Department of Labor, Bureau of Labor Statistics. Local figures are readily available from state bureaus of employment security, and each agency usually maintains a library, which you may use for back issues if your local library does not carry them. The U.S. Department of Labor maintains regional centers as well, through which these and several following cited statistics may also be referenced.

Why know these figures? Your community, board of trustees, fellow administrators, students, and you need to understand existing perceptions and beliefs, as compared to the real world. This author comes from a multicampus district in which these realities have very difficult effects on colleges, depending directly on the communities they serve and the unemployment found in each of the communities. These figures are further broken down into eight major industrial categories, with a total of thirty-two major and subcategories statistically reported. The major categories are mining; construction; manufacturing—durable goods; manufacturing—nondurable goods; transportation and public utilities; wholesale trade; retail trade; finance, insurance, and real estate; and services. Some of these, when reviewed for local implications, may become even more valuable to the interests served by your college.

Federal, State, and Local Employment Projections

New programs usually require the investment of many dollars. High-technology programs require the latest delivery systems. The most obvious need usually centers on equipment and staff. Some needs may lead to the construction of new buildings designed specifically to serve a given program or set of programs. Industry may be approached to contribute not only the time and salaries of those who serve at advisory board meetings but also, in some instances, equipment, in-service training of staff, and even summer employment for staff, for firsthand updating.

Information on these areas of job growth is found through the federal and state agencies for labor statistics. The U.S. Bureau of Labor Statistics has just published employment projections to 1995. To compile these statistics, state counterparts for labor statistics need to conduct their own studies and resultant projections to pass on to the federal agency. State agencies use identical occupational categories, although their published lists may be more extensive than the federal one, given knowledge of local areas and comparisons to the national figures. Your state agency can give you not only state projections but also usually projections for the county or counties served by your college. In addition, if you work in a metropolitan area, you may find the state agency cooperating with one or more concerned city agencies and/or chambers of commerce to bring these figures into finer focus.

Unfortunately, these reports are listed by a predetermined ordering of employment categories, as found repeatedly in other Bureau of Labor

Statistics reports. This ordering is not associated with the order of projected growth. It therefore becomes necessary to seek out from these reports the rank order by projected growth. It must also be remembered that there is nothing sacred about these projections. They are guideposts to be used to point us toward industries believed to have the greatest growth potential between the time of the report and the targeted year of the study. Here is an example of the need for caution. The federal government predicted an annual addition to the work force of 22,990 licensed practical nurses (Pilot, 1982). In two subsequent reports (Silvestri and Lukasiewicz, 1985; and Kahl and Clark, 1986), annual growth for LPNs is listed as 9,636, a reduction of 13,354 per year. Nine months later, a revised 1995 projection listed the annual growth rate for LPNs as 6,483. Kahl and Clark point out, in part: "Increased public and private sector emphasis on health care cost containment is the most important development in recent years. Health economists and policy makers had long been concerned about rapidly rising health care expenditures, but it was not until the early 1980s that the combined impact of inflation, recession, soaring outlays for employee health benefits, threatened Medicare insolvency, and state fiscal crises produced significant action by business, labor, and government. . . . Cost containment initiatives figure prominently among the reasons for a recent decline in hospital employment. . . . More than 73,000 hospital jobs disappeared in 1984, and 37,000 more in 1985 (p. 27-28)."

No one can guarantee the future, but by taking these projections and establishing strong ties with top-growth industries, one can begin to find out about the local implications of these projections and the need for new or expanded programs in these areas.

Periodicals, Newspapers, and Government Publications

Business periodicals are an important source of information that should be consulted along with government data. *Business Week* features a section called "Business Outlook" that keeps one tuned to developments in the business world, such as in manufacturing and the service industries and their effects on the economy. Imports, foreign trade, and foreign manufacturing competition in overseas markets are also recurring topics. Another excellent periodical is *High Technology*, which presents articles on this ever-growing, changing, and redefined area of our nation's businesses. In addition, there are several publications, such as *Crane's Chicago Business*, that cover trends in local economics. Quite often, local newspapers publish in-depth series addressing local economic changes.

One can also monitor Sunday job ads in local newspapers. This author, using federal, state, and local employment projections, identified twenty-six employment categories projected to experience growth. These have now been monitored for 115 consecutive weeks. They support twenty-four and reject two of these projections to date. Interestingly, the 1995 projections have altered the figures, especially for the latter two categories, which now reflect the job-ad "action" 100 percent. In addition, now that these categories have been counted weekly and computerized, a graphic representation may be studied for each category and begins to suggest that the peak hiring times of the year do not coincide with our school terms, being at a low point when we are graduating our hopeful and aspiring students.

Finally, seek out your U.S. Government Regional Bookstore and get on its mailing list, not only for general publications of the Superintendent of Documents but also for topical mailings. In addition, contact your regional offices of both the U.S. Department of Labor, Bureau of Labor Statistics, and the U.S. Department of Commerce and request being placed on appropriate mailing lists. Discuss your needs with the representatives who field telephone calls so that you can receive timely publications on the ever-changing economy and its impact on present and future employment.

For example, did you know that prime working-age women are expected to account for more than one-third of the labor force in 1995, and that the gap between male and female participation has been diminishing and is projected to continue to narrow at least through 1995? You would have known if you had read the *Monthly Labor Review* (Fullerton, 1985). Could you use this information along with, say, the unemployed female single-parent statistics for your area to establish the bases of need for a drop-off center rather than an all-day child-care center to support your occupational programs? Also, did you know that the Community College of Baltimore has formed a partnership with the Youth Services Corporation and its Job Training Program to provide entrepreneural education to 6,000 young people? This was reported in *Minority Business Today* ("Partnership Program . . . ," 1986), a publication of the Minority Business Development Agency of the U.S. Department of Commerce.

Emerging Occupational Categories

If you review federal and state employment projections, you will soon note that no effort has been made to identify new and emerging occupations as separate, distinct employment categories. Thus, openings for computer axial tomography technologists, cyberneticists, energy auditors and conservation technicians, laser calibration technicians, microcomputer diagnosticians, ocean robotics specialists, positron emission technologists, and telemarketers and teletext broadcasters are never identified, and one can only assume that these occupations have been included under an existing and more general category. We are told that this shortcoming should be corrected somewhat in the 1987 reports, at least some of them. How, then, can one become conversant with emerging areas of employment so that one can identify businesses and industries to be queried for projected training needs? This author has turned to the futurists for some of these insights. Several excellent resources can be very helpful in these efforts. Cetron and Appel (1984), for example, reference 500 jobs, both traditional and emerging, with a complete national occupational profile section, which considers such topics as projection of workers required by 1990, projected annual salaries, projected rate of growth (from obsolescence to new), perceived educational level required for employment, and work site or mode (office, mobile, home, and so forth). Feingold and Miller (1983) identify and briefly describe many future occupations, although they do not give the kinds of number projections that can help one begin to identify industries that may be hiring, training, or developing responsibilities in these new vocational areas.

Membership in the World Future Society brings the new member a gift (at least at the time of this writing), *Careers Tomorrow: The Outlook for Work in a Changing World*. In addition, one receives the society's bimonthly magazine, *The Futurist*, which combines forecasts, trends, and ideas about the future in such areas as communications, demographics, education, health, science, technology, and work. The society's Futurist Bookstore stores over 250 discounted books, audiotapes, and other materials that deal with the future. Of course, not all these books focus on jobs. If you become really involved in the activities of this organization, you can join a regional group and attend the annual national conference to meet those who have already identified techniques for projecting that may help you expand your approach to the programs of the future for your institution.

Industrial associations may be another excellent source of information on new and emerging occupational responsibilities in members' businesses, manufacturing plants, or shops. Responses from the staffs of these associations vary, depending on the identified responsibilities and commitments each association has established through its membership. This author has had excellent assistance from a number of these associations, including contact with local members, who have proved most helpful on developmental advisory boards. A very good reference to over 6,000 national trade associations, labor unions, and professional, scientific, and technical societies is the *National Trade & Professional Associations of the United States Directory*, published by Columbia Books, Inc., Suite 207, 1350 New York Avenue N.W., Washington, D.C. 20005.

Projections for New Industries by State and Local Agencies

National, state, and local governmental employment statistical agencies have already been mentioned. Serious developers should search out other governmental agencies that may enhance the findings of those mentioned above. In Illinois, the home of this author, several such agencies monitor the development and well-being of fledgling businesses in local communities. To find such agencies in your state, look for key identifiers like chambers of commerce, departments of commerce and community affairs and economic development, state occupational information coordinating committees, local planning commissions, state university departments of research, state boards of adult and vocational education, offices of employment and training, city commercial clubs, and, of course, local and county boards of education. Each of these has unique contributions to help you. Who could better know the training needs of new industry moving into your state than the state department of commerce and community affairs?

Sources for Industrial Surveys

Nothing can replace a survey of existing local business or industry (identified through the foregoing processes) for a final understanding of your area's specific growth potentials. This survey must include businesses within commuting distance, as developing opportunities are so often in someone else's "back yard." One should acquire a market identifier for each employment category under consideration. This document usually includes businesses listed by name with complete addresses, telephone numbers, current number of employees, names of chief executive officers and personnel directors, and, most important, Standard Industrial Classification (SIC) code. Three sources of these identifiers are the Dun & Bradstreet Corporation's Dun's Marketing Services Division, Three Century Drive, Parsippany, NJ 07054; Harris Publishing Company, 2057-2 Aurora Road, Twinsburg, OH 44087; and Manufacturers' News, Inc., 4 East Huron Street, Chicago, IL 60611. These companies also furnish computer listings of given industries, which may be sorted by their zip or SIC codes. These reports are expensive but may save time. The SIC system was developed by the federal government and divides all economic activity into ten major divisions, with four-digit codes:

Agriculture, forestry, and fishing	(01-09)
Mining	(10-14)
Construction	(15-17)
Manufacturing	(20-39)
Transportation, communication, and public utilities	(40-49)
Wholesale trade	(50-51)
Retail trade	(52-59)
Finance, insurance, and real-estate services	(60-67)
Business services	(70-89)
Health/social services and public administration	(91-97)

The first two digits of each code relate to the broad area of the business. The third and fourth digits identify the specific industry. For example:

22   Manufacturing—textile mill products
227   Manufacturing—floor coverings
2272 Manufacturing—tufted carpets, rugs

An additional listing is now available. This listing identifies each employment category contained in your state's employment projections report within each SIC code for which your state identifies existing industries. It can be obtained from your state's occupational informational coordinating committee. By combining the above two reports (a time-consuming task), one can focus on industries (in particular zip codes) that employ individuals in the job classifications expected to experience the most growth between now and 1995.

Advisory Committees

If you have spent the hours necessary to accomplish the thorough research suggested here and have concluded that the program under consideration has displayed enough positive indicators to have you convene an advisory committee, then you can very easily forget that this committee is to be your local barometer of actual success. Consequently, you may try to sell this group of knowledgeable professionals something they should reject. The advisory committee is your ultimate resource for needs assessment. Just as so many weekend amateur home-maintenance workers misuse their tools, so can the amateur program researcher misuse a program feasibility advisory committee. You must keep in mind that a group like this usually is flattered that you have taken such an interest in their profession. They may also be skeptical of your knowledge of their industry. If you come to them in the beginning with a strong sales pitch, instead of an agenda that seeks insightful help from these practitioners, their local companies, and their parent corporations, you may very well conclude your meeting with an agreement to develop a program for which there are no local needs and, more important, no jobs. If however, the need for a program has been clearly established, you are then able to have additional meetings with this advisory committee for the purpose of developing the curriculum.

References

Cetron, M., and Appel, M. *Jobs of the Future.* New York: McGraw-Hill, 1984.
Feingold, N., and Miller, N. *Engineering Careers: New Occupations for the Year 2000 and Beyond.* Garrett Park, Md.: Garrett Park Press, 1983.
Fullerton, H. N., Jr. "The 1995 Labor Force: BLS' Latest Projections." *Monthly Labor Review,* 1985, *108* (11), 17-25.

Kahl, A., and Clark, D. E. "Employment in Health Services: Long-Term Trends and Projections." *Monthly Labor Review,* 1986, *109* (8), 17-36.

"Partnership Program Motivates Youth to Pursue Business Careers." *Minority Business Today,* 1986, *5* (2), p. 1.

Pilot, M. (ed.). *Occupational Projections and Training Data.* Washington, D.C.: Government Printing Office, 1982.

Silvestri, G. T., and Lukasiewicz, J. M. "Occupational Employment Projections: The 1984-95 Outlook." *Monthly Labor Review,* 1985, *108* (11), 42-57.

Donald B. Smith is executive dean for skills programs at the City Colleges of Chicago. He served as president of the National Council for Occupational Education in 1982-83.

Everyone on campus is affected by accreditation.

Accrediting Occupational Programs

Roland V. Stoodley, Jr.

Educational accreditation in the United States has become a very important factor for educational institutions. The system is designed to recognize these institutions and various programs within institutions as meeting a level of performance, integrity, and quality that inspires confidence in the education community and the public it serves. The uniqueness of the American system is that it is nongovernmental, unlike systems in the many countries that have established ministries of education to oversee and supervise offerings. Voluntary in nature, the accreditation system is based on the work of various accrediting associations, which are responsible for establishing criteria for accreditation, arranging site visits, evaluating institutions that desire accredited status, and publishing lists of institutions and programs that meet certain minimum standards established by the criteria.

The purpose of this chapter is to provide a broad outline of the accreditation process as it concerns occupational education. The individual who develops the curriculum must make certain that the institution complies with the standards of the accrediting agency and that the agency is involved in the initial planning.

This chapter contains key accreditation terminology within explanations of articulation, accreditation classifications, standards for accreditation, self-study (including a Program Evaluation and Review Technique,

PERT, chart of accreditation activities), and site visits. In addition, addresses of major accrediting associations are given, and sources in the ERIC system and literature are provided.

Process of Accreditation

Accreditation is a process by which an institution of postsecondary education periodically evaluates its educational activities, in whole or in part, and seeks an independent judgment that it substantially achieves its own educational objectives and is generally equal in quality to comparable institutions or specialized units. Essential elements of the process are a clear statement of educational objectives, a directed self-study focused on these objectives, an on-site evaluation by a selected group of peers, and a decision by an independent commission that the institution or specialized unit is worthy of accreditation.

Accrediting Body. An accrediting body is a voluntary, nongovernmental association established to administer accrediting procedures. A *recognized* accrediting body is one that is formally acknowledged by the Council on Postsecondary Accreditation (COPA) as having met COPA's provisions and procedures for recognition. A *listed* accrediting body is one that is officially listed by the Secretary of Education because it is utilized as part of the Department of Education's processes for determining institutional eligibility for certain federal funds.

Institutional Accreditation. Institutional accreditation is a status of affiliation accorded by an accrediting body to an institution of postsecondary education. Such accreditation embraces the totality of the institution as it defines itself. Institutional accreditation determines that each part of the institution is contributing to the achievement of the institution's educational objectives but does not necessarily evaluate specific units or programs. *Regional* accrediting bodies accredit a variety of institutions in three or more states. *National* accrediting bodies accredit institutions of a certain kind in many states.

Regional Institutional Accrediting Bodies

>   Middle States Association of Colleges and Schools
>   Commission on Higher Education
>   3624 Market Street
>   Philadelphia, Pennsylvania 19104

>   New England Association of Schools and Colleges
>   Commission on Institutions of Higher Education
>   Commission on Vocational, Technical, Career Institutions
>   The Sanborn House, 15 High Street
>   Winchester, Massachusetts 01890

North Central Association of Colleges and Schools
Commission on Institutions of Higher Education
159 North Dearborn Street
Chicago, Illinois 60601

Northwest Association of Schools and Colleges
Commission on Colleges
3700-B University Way N.E.
Seattle, Washington 98105

Southern Association of Colleges and Schools
Commission on Colleges
Commission on Occupational Education Institutions
759 Peachtree Street N.E.
Atlanta, Georgia 30365

Western Association of Schools and Colleges
Accrediting Commission for Senior Colleges and Universities
c/o Mills College, Box 9990
Oakland, California 94613

Accrediting Commission for Community and Junior Colleges
P.O. Box 70
9053 Soquel Drive
Aptos, California 95003

In addition to the six regional accrediting associations, there are four national institutional accrediting agencies.

American Association of Bible Colleges
Box 1523
130-F North College Street
Fayetteville, Arkansas 72701

Association of Independent Schools and Colleges
Accrediting Commission
One Dupont Circle, Suite 350
Washington, D.C. 20036

National Association of Trade and Technical Schools
Accrediting Commission
2021 K Street N.W., Room 305
Washington, D.C. 20006

National Home Study Council
Accrediting Commission
1601 Eighteenth Street N.W.
Washington, D.C. 20009

Accreditation Classifications

Accreditation is a status granted an institution or specialized unit that has undergone the accrediting process and has been judged to meet or exceed general expectations of education quality.

Candidacy for Accreditation. Candidacy for accreditation is a status that may be granted by an accrediting body to indicate that an institution or unit has expressed its desire to become accredited and that the accrediting body judges the institution or unit to have the potential for achieving accreditation within a reasonable period, normally a maximum of six years. Candidacy, however, does not ensure accreditation. (This status may also be referred to as preaccreditation status.)

Conditional Accreditation. Conditional accreditation is a status indicating that an institution or a unit has certain deficiencies that must be corrected within a specific period of time in order for the institution or unit to remain accredited. (While some accrediting bodies may make certain distinctions among these terms, conditional accreditation may also be referred to as *probationary* or *provisional accreditation*.)

Specialized Accreditation. Specialized accreditation is a status of affiliation accorded by an accrediting body to a special unit within an institution of postsecondary education, such as a college, school, division, department, program, or curriculum. In some instances, freestanding specialized institutions also receive specialized accreditation.

Standards for Accreditation

Institutional. Each commission of the accrediting agency publishes standards of membership. These standards indicate to the institution the items upon which the commission will base its findings once the accreditation process (application, self-study, site visit) is complete. The standards also will assist the institution to improve the quality of education it offers. An example of headings for the standards of membership of a commission follows.

- Purposes and objectives
- Control and administration
- Finance
- Students
- Program of studies
- Physical plant

- Learning centers (library)
- Publications, public announcements, public relations
- General (any other relevant subjects)

Programmatic. In programmatic accreditation, there also exist standards for accreditation, although the standards are more uniformly termed *essentials*. The essentials for program accreditation tend to direct themselves to specific program components, rather than to the institution as a whole. In many cases, however, institutional accreditation is a requirement for program accreditation. Such institutional accreditation could be granted by a recognized national accrediting association, such as the National Association of Trade and Technical Schools, rather than by one of the six regional accrediting agencies.

Below are example headings for the essentials of a program.

- Educational institutions
- Clinical affiliations
- Facilities
- Finances
- Faculty
- Advisory committee
- Students
- Records
- Curriculum
- Administration
- Accreditation information
- Summary and conclusions

The Self-Study

"The institutional self-study is a comprehensive analysis of the educational resources and effectiveness of an institution or specialized unit in relation to its educational objectives. The results of this process are called the self-study report or educational statement. The self-study is the most important part of the accrediting process, and the self-study report is the essential document in the process" (Council on Postsecondary Accreditation, 1980, p. 4).

Institutional self-study, as defined by the Commission on Colleges, Northwest Association of Schools and Colleges (NWASC), should be an ongoing process for purposes of improvement. Whether used for accreditation or other purposes, it is an analysis of the institution's resources and effectiveness by its own staff. The aim must be to understand, evaluate, and improve, not merely to defend what already exists (Northwest Association of Schools and Colleges, 1978).

Kells (1977) maintains that self-study is a process, not a document. Misunderstanding of this distinction has too often led to the distortion of self-study activity toward the production of an unwieldy tome; but many self-studies also serve as first steps in the accreditation review process. For this and occasionally other purposes, the self-study should produce a readable document for the visiting team or other group, both as an introduction to the college and as a summary of the problems, strengths, recent actions, activities, and probable steps to be taken as a result of the self-study.

The preliminary phase of the self-study starts with a form request for accreditation or reaccreditation by the chief administrative officer, or the designee, to the respective accrediting agency. This is followed by the agency's taking necessary action and, if the request is for initial accreditation, appointing a committee to visit the institution and report on the institution's status for candidacy. Candidacy status permits an institution to proceed with the self-study. The institution is then ready for appointment of a steering committee, a self-study committee, and subcommittees (see Figure 1). The self-study plan is developed, and informational meetings are conducted to brief staff, administrators, governing board, and advisory committee members.

The various subcommittees conduct a self-study of units within the institution, based on the steering committee's plan and on guidelines from the accrediting agency. As each report is completed, it is reviewed by the steering committee and eventually by the staff of the institution. It is the responsibility of the steering committee to keep the process moving at a pace that will enable timely completion of the reports. For this reason, a plan should include target dates, such as those suggested in Figure 1. As reports are submitted, they are reviewed for accuracy by each subcommittee prior to becoming part of the final self-study draft. Upon completion of all subcommittee reports, the steering committee produces the final draft report of the institution, at which time the report is reviewed by the staff, administration, governing board, and advisory committees. The final report is then printed and is ready for submission to the accrediting agency.

The completion phase involves submitting the institutional self-study report to the accrediting agency and preparing for the visit of a team of individuals from institutions accredited by the agency. The institutional self-study report is made available to the visiting committee members well in advance of their visit.

The following outline of steps to be followed in conducting a self-study for institutional accreditation corresponds to the tasks illustrated in the PERT chart in Figure 1.

Reaccreditation

1. One year before renewal of accreditation, contact accrediting agency.
2. Accrediting agency commission director forwards necessary materials for start of self-study.
3. Chief administrative officer (CAO) meets with administrative council (staff) to plan self-study.
4. Commission director may meet with institution staff for discussion.

Figure 1. Suggested PERT for Two-Year Postsecondary Accreditation Self-Study Process

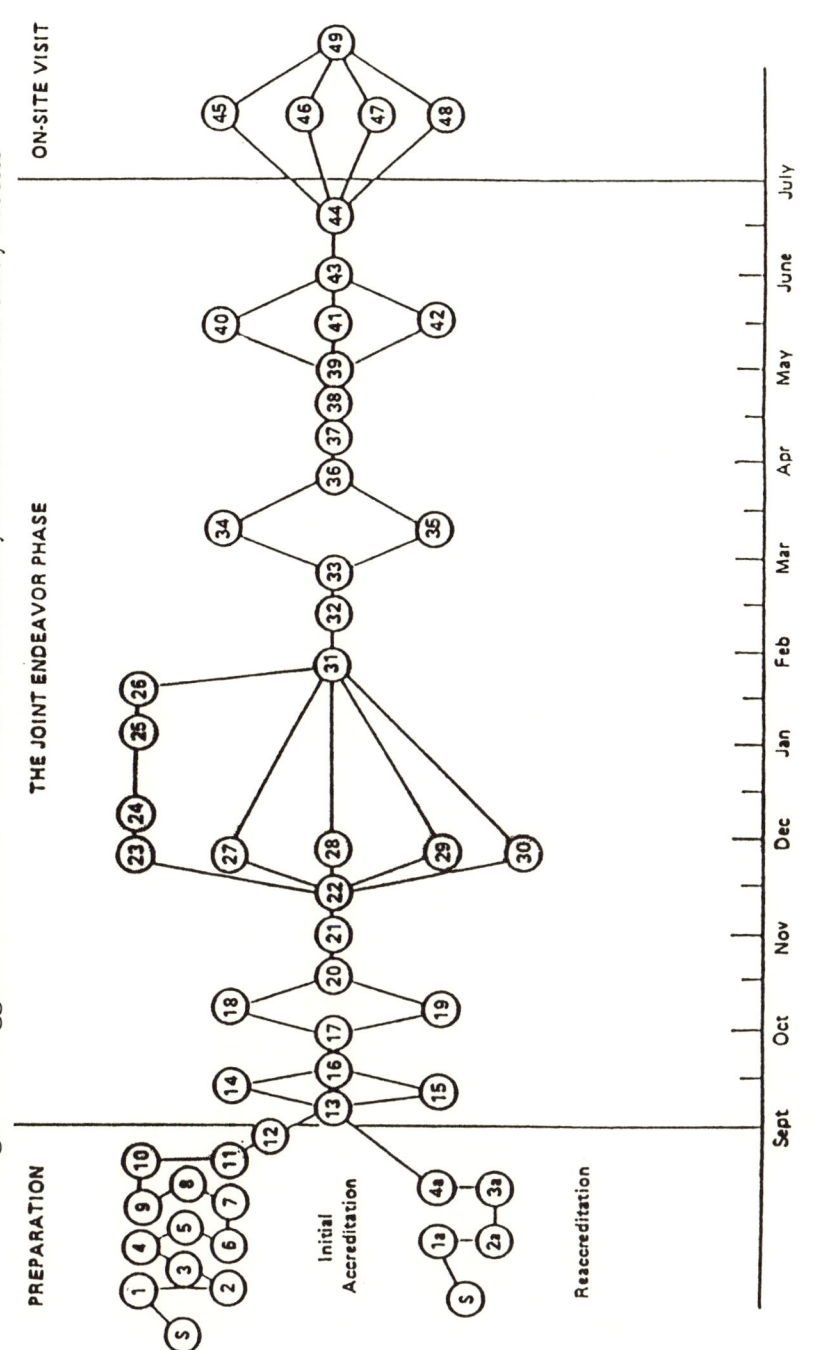

Source: Stoodley, 1982.

Initial Accreditation

1. CAO decides to implement accreditation.
2. Letter of request for accreditation is sent to accrediting agency.
3. Agency responds by sending preaccreditation materials.
4. CAO or designee completes data sheet.
5. Data sheet and other required materials returned to agency.
6. Agency commission director submits request and materials at commission meeting.
7. Commission director may request additional materials at commission meeting.
8. Commission director may appoint one or two individuals to visit the institution for a look at general operations.
9. Individuals report back to the commission director.
10. Commission director submits materials to the commission meeting for vote of preaccreditation (candidacy) status.
11. Commission director notifies the CAO of results.
12. CAO meets with administrative council to announce accreditation status and decide on the next steps to take (time limit of this status depends on the agency).
13. Steering committee chairperson is appointed.
14. CAO meets with chairperson to discuss strategies.
15. Steering committee is selected.
16. Steering committee meets to discuss accreditation.
17. Data sheets, other handout information materials, and formats to use in self-study are prepared.
18. Steering committee meets to discuss and approve materials and format structure.
19. All staff meet for orientation/in-service on the self-study process.
20. Steering committee meets to develop the self-study plan.
21. Steering committee meets to select subcommittee chairpersons and members.
22. Steering committee meets with subcommittee chairpersons to discuss strategies, procedures, and deadlines and give out materials.
23. Subcommittees meet to plan their self-study.
24. Subcommittees perform their self-study.
25. Subcommittees meet to discuss results of the self-study and vote on accepting report.
26. Subcommittees submit their self-study report to the steering committee.
27. Steering committee chairperson meets with the governing board to discuss the accreditation process.
28. Steering committee chairperson meets with institutional advisory board to discuss accreditation process.

29. Steering committee chairperson meets with administrative council (staff) to discuss accreditation progress.
30. Steering committee gathers all internal reports, printed materials, and documents pertinent to the self-study.
31. Steering committee meets with subcommittee chairperson to discuss reports.
32. Steering committee votes on acceptance of each subcommittee report.
33. Steering committee meets to assemble draft copy of institutional self-study report.
34. Steering committee votes on acceptance of draft report.
35. Draft report is discussed and voted on at all-staff meeting.
36. Draft report is presented to administrative council (staff) for review and comments.
37. Steering committee meets to revise self-study report draft.
38. Steering committee meets to vote on final self-study report.
39. Self-study report is printed.
40. Staff meets to distribute self-study report and discuss next steps in accreditation.
41. Self-study report presented and discussed at meeting of governing board.
42. Self-study report presented and discussed at meeting of institutional advisory council.
43. Self-study report presented and discussed at meeting of administrative council (staff).
44. Self-study report submitted to COA for expediting to accrediting agency.
45. Steering committee meets to prepare for the site visit.
46. Administrative council (staff) meets to develop plan of action for institutional improvement based on results of self-study.
47. Steering committee chairperson arranges accommodations for visiting committee.
48. Steering committee chairperson gathers pertinent materials for visiting committee.
49. Site visit.

The Site Visit

Upon submission of the self-study report to the agency, the institution or program prepares for the site visit. Materials and documents used by the institution are gathered and made ready for the visit. These include but are not limited to:
1. Authorization and/or statutes for the establishment of the institution

2. List of governing board, faculty, and staff advisory committee members
3. Statement of purposes and objectives of the institution
4. Faculty, student, and other handbooks
5. Floor plans
6. Contractual agreement on the salary schedule
7. Descriptive institutional materials
8. Various reports (budget, admissions, placement)
9. Faculty/class schedules
10. Personnel policies and procedures (Stoodley, 1982).

The visiting committee consists of peers selected by the association who are from member institutions that are already accredited. The heart of the voluntary accreditation process is evaluation by peers who are qualified in their fields and who can bring to the educational process an objectivity that is not readily available within, between, and among members of an institution (Hamel, 1976). Depending on the institution to be accredited, the team consists of from five to twenty-five members. It usually spends three or four days observing operations, meeting institutional representatives and students, touring facilities, and reviewing documents. The self-study guide, which visiting team members receive several weeks before the visit, is useful for evaluating various aspects of the institution.

The visiting committee meets as a body to review recommendations, submits its findings, and discusses the institution as a whole. Although the committee chairperson is responsible for the final report, it should reflect the consensus of the total committee and contain an evaluation report of the committee as a whole. In many situations, each item of the report is voted on by the entire visiting committee. After the visit, an exit interview is held. Those invited are selected by the CAO. What happens at the exit interview is up to the visiting committee chairperson and may or may not touch on the detailed findings of the visit. The final report is written by the chairperson of the visiting committee and then submitted to the CAO for review of accuracy. Nothing may be changed in the body of the report. The report is now ready to be considered by the regional commission.

Summary

In an age of accountability, program quality is paramount. Educational quality is enhanced by self-study and peer evaluation. Accreditation is ongoing and does not stop after the site visit. Perhaps the most interesting aspect of accreditation in the United States is that it is voluntary and nongovernmental. Accreditation is needed and will be with us for a long time. A major issue is whether it will remain voluntary or whether government will gradually take it over.

References

Council on Postsecondary Accreditation. *A Glossary of Preferred Terms in the Accreditation of Postsecondary Education.* Washington, D.C.: Council on Postsecondary Accreditation, 1980.

Hamel, D. B. "The Importance of Accreditation." Remarks at the annual meeting of the Southern Association of Colleges and Schools, Atlanta, Ga., 1976.

Kells, H. R. "An Alternative Model for Self-Study in Higher Education." *North Central Association Quarterly,* 1977, *52,* 341-346.

Northwest Association of Schools and Colleges. *Accreditation Handbook—Commission on Colleges.* Seattle, Wash.: Northwest Association of Schools and Colleges, 1978.

Stoodley, R. V., Jr. "The Development and Evaluation of a Single Self-Study Method for Use in Two-Year Postsecondary Institution and Multi-Program Accreditation." Doctoral dissertation, University of Minnesota, 1982.

Ronald V. Stoodley, Jr., is president of the New Hampshire Vocational-Technical College at Claremont. He has served as president of the New England Association of Schools and Colleges, Inc., and on the board of the Council on Postsecondary Accreditation for five years.

This chapter reviews the basic concepts of licensing and certification, noting their importance to the curriculum development process.

What Teachers and Administrators Need to Know About Licensing and Certification Tests

Charles J. Teryek

Most occupational licensing and certification requires some type of testing. As testing gains wider acceptance in the credentialing process, vocational educators will need to understand basic occupational testing concepts so that they can better prepare students for the transition from the classroom to the world of work. Further, rapidly changing technology and the trend toward consumerism raise questions about the wisdom of credentialing an individual for life. Recredentialing often requires retraining. Therefore, vocational educators are logically the indicated designers and providers of the delivery system for continuing occupational education.

The Need to Know About Occupational Tests

There is a definite trend toward reliance on regulation of job entry and of the evaluation of continued competency of job incumbents. At the turn of the century, very few occupations were regulated. Since the early 1900s, the number of occupations subject to regulation by local, state, or national governmental agencies has risen to more than 800 (Shimberg, 1984). Testing, most often in the form of multiple-choice written tests, is the usual method for credentialing.

In both licensure and certification testing (a discussion of the differences between licensing and certification appears later), the issue of content validity is the part of the process most likely to provoke costly and time-consuming litigation.

To reduce the possibility of litigation, credentialing agencies are becoming more inclined to use tests that are nationally accepted and developed by independent testing companies. Nationally developed tests are more likely to have content based on properly documented and legally defensible job analyses. Tests developed exclusively by board members of licensing or certification agencies, who generally have little or no test-development skill, are becoming less common.

While these boards generally control the supply of credentialed individuals, the public generally affects both supply and demand. Licensed or certified individuals are, in the public eye, associated with a higher quality of skill and service. By demanding the services of these individuals, the public influences the supply.

Professional and trade groups also affect the supply of credentialed individuals. Indeed, most early licensure in the United States evolved through the efforts of professionals seeking job security and higher pay. Limiting the supply of licensed individuals in certain occupations was achieved by creating artificially high licensing standards. Fewer licenses meant more business for those who were licensed. Studies by Gellhorn (1976) and Rayack (1976) appear to confirm that this approach persists today. More recently, craftsmen and others have capitalized on the professional image associated with being credentialed, and the result is national credentialing programs for such groups as auto mechanics, dance exercise instructors, business forms consultants, moving consultants, and others.

Historically, vocational educators prepared candidates for the needs of the local work force and overlooked nationally accepted job requirements. Educators often relied on their own judgment and experience when deciding what to teach. This subjective approach to selecting course content sometimes resulted in students leaving training improperly prepared and unable to demonstrate that they possessed the knowledge necessary to enter the national work force. Different programs that train individuals for the same credential continue to vary significantly, depending on the instructor, the type of training institution, or the location of the training. For example, to be certified as a food service manager in Florida, three hours of training are required, followed by successful completion of a one-hour state-developed test. The same certification in Illinois requires fifteen hours of training followed by successful completion of either a state test or a test developed by one of two national testing organizations.

In both states, prospective food service managers who were trained in other states or in corporations or institutions must take state-offered training. Reciprocity, in which one state accepts the credential of another, is not in effect between Florida and Illinois.

To deal with this type of disparity and training redundancy for food service managers, the United States Food and Drug Administration (FDA) promoted the use of a single job-related national test that was developed and administered by an independent third-party evaluator. As a result of FDA's action, vocational educators, trainers in corporate settings, and entrepreneurs who offer training for food service managers must know the national standards and they must train their students to meet those standards.

From the foregoing discussion, which identifies the need for a close match between curriculum and test content, educators may erroneously conclude that all that is needed is wholesale preparation of candidates to pass tests. Nothing could be farther from the truth. Although preparation for occupational tests is helpful, it is not intended as a replacement for sound training on job principles and skills. It is clear that properly designed training imparts job knowledge and generates skills, abilities, and personal characteristics that are not measured by occupational tests.

In summary, it is vitally important for vocational educators to understand the purpose of licensing and certification examinations. The national trend is toward greater reliance on tests by regulators. Individuals seeking training to enter the world of work, as well as those in need of retraining, will increasingly demand that they be properly prepared for national tests. Vocational curricula will need to be adjusted to meet knowledge and skill standards determined by nationally recognized authorities.

Differences Between Licensing and Certification

Grimm (1972) reports that in many states in the early part of the nineteenth century, almost anyone could use the title of physician and practice medicine without legal restrictions. Large numbers of poorly prepared individuals were graduated from more than 150 training schools established to meet the demand for medical training. The abundance of poorly prepared physicians caused considerable public and professional concern. State governments, working with the American Medical Association (AMA), enacted medical practice laws, making it illegal to practice without a license. The AMA's desire to prevent quacks and charlatans from entering the profession led to the profession's strong support for licensure (Shimberg, 1984).

Other professional groups quickly recognized the monetary benefits of a favorable public image generated by licensure. By the early 1960s, the combination of professional desire and public need resulted in the licensing of approximately twenty different occupations in most states. The concept of licensure as a form of consumer protection generated renewed public interest in the 1970s, and licensing activity peaked as legislation was enacted to license additional tradesmen and professionals.

The original purpose of licensure was to restrict practice—to make it illegal to practice without a license. Practice was restricted by licensing boards that identified the minimum competencies a licensed individual needed to protect the public from harm. This concept continues to be crucial to licensing, and the United States Department of Health, Education and Welfare (1971) issued the following definition: *"Licensure:* The process by which an agency of government grants permission to persons to engage in a given profession or occupation by certifying that those licensed have attained the minimal degree of competency necessary to ensure that the public health, safety and welfare will be reasonably well protected" (p. 7).

Several studies conducted in the late 1960s and the early 1970s by the Department of Labor, the Federal Trade Commission, and the Department of Justice highlighted the negative impact that licensure could have on manpower needs and mobility (Shimberg, 1984). These inquiries led to greater public awareness of licensing and to the development of a more critical scheduled review of licensing activities at the state level, through what is now called sunset legislation. Most licensing boards whose activities have been reviewed as a result of this legislation have withstood the rigorous process because (in this writer's opinion) the benefits of licensure continue to outweigh the drawbacks.

Certification also began as a result of concerns within the professions. For example, the need for recognition of competence, above the minimum level required for licensure, resulted in the formation of a certification board by the American Ophthalmic Society. In 1916, this nongovernmental professional agency offered its first certification test in an attempt to encourage ophthalmologists to obtain additional training after licensure. Two significant principles—the demonstration of competence above the minimum level required to protect the public, and control of the demonstration process by a nongovernmental agency—emerged from this early certification process.

The United States Department of Health, Education and Welfare's (1971) definition of certification is as follows: *"Certification:* The process by which a nongovernmental agency or association grants recognition to an individual who has met certain predetermined qualifications specified by the agency or association. Such qualifications may include graduation from an accredited or approved training program, acceptable performance on a qualifying examination, and/or completion of some specified amount or type of work experience" (p. 7).

While licensing tests were primarily designed to identify practitioners who possess the minimum acceptable level of competence, certification tests, in contrast, were primarily designed to test at some higher level of competence. This difference in purpose, although initially quite distinct, has become less obvious as licensing and certification programs have increased. Specialty certification for expertise continues to be awarded by more than fifty medical boards. Many certification bodies, however, such as the Professional Picture Framers of America, the American Electrologist Association, and the American Institute of Planners, award certification status for demonstration of minimum competence.

Whether preparing students for licensure or certification, the vocational educator has similar concerns. Course content must reflect actual required job knowledge, skills, and abilities; students must be taught to demonstrate that they have acquired the necessary knowledge, skills, and abilities to perform the job without harming the public; and students must be prepared to demonstrate that they understand how the laws, rules, and regulations of the credentialing agency affect the job.

Relicensure and Recertification

Historically, licensing and certification boards have been concerned only with determining job-entry competence. Once an individual was licensed or certified, the credential was assumed to be valid for life. Boards rarely checked to see if credentialed individuals maintained the mental and physical qualities necessary to perform the job safely (Shimberg, 1982).

More recently, boards have become concerned about the need to determine continued competence. Rapidly changing technology and the introduction of new tools, techniques, and materials have caused board members to question the time-honored belief that increased years of experience automatically provide increased quality and provision of up-to-date service.

Several strategies have been developed to deal with this concern. They include continuing education, various forms of retesting, and, to a lesser extent, peer review of a relicensure candidate's job practice. A summary of only the examination process will be given here.

The concept of reexamination has not been enthusiastically endorsed everywhere. Credentialed individuals resist it because they believe that the tests, which usually test general job knowledge, are not appropriate for practitioners who specialize in particular fields. Boards tend to resist recredentialing because of the enormous financial, manpower, and policing burdens it places on already overburdened credentialing systems. Many critics simply argue that relicensing and recertification strategies are inappropriate because the problem is not the lack of job knowledge possessed by credentialed individuals, but rather their failure to use the knowledge properly because of greed, physical or emotional problems, substance abuse, and other problems. They believe that stricter enforcement is needed to weed out poor performers and that it is not necessary to burden the majority of credentialed individuals who are performing adequately.

Consequently, Shimberg (1981) reported that no state required reexamination as a method of relicensure. This continues to be true. Some national certification boards now have recertification requirements, however.

This writer is aware of at least six medical specialty boards that use or are considering the use of written tests for recertification. Of those that use tests, most require it to be taken three to five years after initial certification. Others encourage retesting on a voluntary basis. One credentialing body, the National Institute for Automotive Service Excellence (NIASE), which offers a voluntary certification program, requires those who want to continue displaying the credential to be recertified every six years.

Types of Occupational Tests

Credentialing boards most often use written, oral, and performance tests. The decision about which type of test to use is based on how well the test measures critical elements of the occupation being tested (Fortune and Associates, 1985). For example, performance tests—observing and evaluating a candidate who physically performs critical and important job tasks, either in a simulated or an actual job setting—are appropriate for a dental hygienist or a plumber but not quite so appropriate for a city planner or an accountant. Frequently, combinations of tests are used, such as written and performance tests for licensure of most barbers and cosmetologists, and written and oral tests for certification of gynecologists.

Each type of test has advantages and disadvantages. Generally, the decision process that a credentialing board uses to select a test is based on measurement concerns, such as validity and reliability, and on practical concerns, such as cost and ease of administration. The Central Testing Unit of the California Department of Consumer Affairs (1983) succinctly points out that unless boards are constantly aware of the distinction between the "ideal" and the "real" when selecting a test, criticism of one type or another is easy. In this writer's opinion, it is also unproductive.

Whether written, oral, or performance tests are used in occupational credentialing, it is essential for vocational educators to understand that test content most often will be based on crucial aspects of a job that must be performed in a manner that will protect the health and safety of the public. Thus, sales techniques, marketing methods, or history of the occupation are skills and knowledge that may be necessary for successfully performing the job, but they are not crucial to protecting the public and therefore are being removed with increasing frequency from standardized occupational credentialing tests.

Concerns for test validity and legal defensibility have resulted in tests based on content identified by formal job analysis. For occupational testing purposes, job analysis, a systematic procedure for identifying what practitioners actually do on the job, is focused on what is important for protecting the public at the entry level only.

Multiple-choice tests are the most widely used type of written test for occupational credentialing. Multiple-choice questions are sometimes grouped into "sets" to test from the same stimuli, such as a reading passage or a diagram. As might be expected, computer technology and latent-image printing have had an impact on this basically simple form of testing, in attempts to increase administrative efficiency and face validity. Sometimes a form of the multiple-choice format—patient-management problems (PMPs)—is used. In this variation of the standard format, a narrative that describes a situation or a series of problems is followed by choices. Each choice leads the candidate through a different course of action, and credit is awarded to the candidate for selecting the most appropriate one.

Critics of this testing format are quick to point out that the format is easily abused and is frequently used to test lower-level recall knowledge only. Proponents, however, argue that properly developed multiple-choice questions can test for fairly sophisticated analysis of ideas, determination of relationships, and application of principles.

Generally, multiple-choice questions can be answered quickly. Thus, more questions can be asked in a given time than with other types of testing. Tests with multiple-choice questions can also be machine-scored, and scores can be reported to candidates quickly. Through the use of clever scrambling and pooling procedures, each test question can be used on a number of different test forms without jeopardizing its security, and test development costs can be minimized.

When seeking licenses or certificates, candidates may encounter essay tests. This format has lost some popularity with credentialing officials because the grading process can be very subjective, cost of scoring can be excessive compared to that for multiple-choice tests, and scoring large numbers of essays requires large amounts of time.

True/false tests are used by some credentialing boards, although infrequently. Therefore, vocational educators should be aware of this format and of the reasons for its use. Many credentialing boards formerly favored this format because test development and scoring is uncomplicated and quickly accomplished. Also, many true/false questions can be presented in a very short time. Professional test makers now avoid this format because of its inherent low reliability and because the probablity of guessing the right answer is higher, .50, as opposed to .20 for a five-choice multiple-choice test.

Some credentialing boards use performance tests to evaluate candidates' skills and abilities. Candidates are observed and evaluated while performing actual job tasks, such as cutting hair or filling cavities. The cost of development, administration, and scoring, as well as the logistics of testing large numbers of candidates, have hindered greater use of this type of test. Inability to standardize testing procedures also frequently yields unreliable test results.

This writer's experience with the development of national performance tests for cosmetologists' and barbers' licensing boards and of an industry-specific test for machine tenders indicates that, with proper care, conditions for development, grading, and administration can be standardized to yield psychometrically sound performance tests.

As the public becomes more concerned about validity, reliability, and legal defensibility of the credentialing process, and as computer technology is applied to testing to reduce costs, performance tests will be the test of choice by many boards who credential occupations that include crucial physical activities.

Preparing for Occupational Tests

An abundance of recent publicity concerning standardized testing has resulted in considerable confusion about the value of preparing for tests. Much of the confusion is caused by advocates of test disclosure, who urge that test makers be legally required to let candidates review copies of test questions and answers after scores are reported. These advocates usually fail to make the distinction between aptitude and achievement tests.

As reported by Pellaton (1980, p. 1), Thorndike states that an aptitude test "undertakes to measure what a person could learn to do, whereas an achievement test measures what he has learned to do. . . . In an aptitude test, our interest is to predict what the individual can learn or develop into in the future; in the achievement test, our interest is in what he has learned in the past."

Licensing and certification tests are designed to measure whether a person has the knowledge and skills necessary to perform the job without harm to the public. These tests are measures of what has been learned in training or through experience. As such, measurement experts agree that occupational tests clearly fit Thorndike's definition of achievement tests (1971). It follows, then, that the more closely training and test content are tied to the job, the better we can expect candidates with training to perform on the test. Thus, training, study, and review for occupational tests are strongly recommended.

In addition to the usual training and subject-matter review that candidates should consider when preparing for occupational tests, they can take a number of other actions before the test to improve scores. Vocational educators and candidates must keep in mind that there is no substitute for knowing the subject matter well. The following suggestions will also help candidates perform to the best of their ability. Although testing programs vary, there is sufficient similarity between them to warrant these suggestions.

Properly developed testing programs will provide candidates with a considerable amount of preparation material, including bulletins or booklets that contain content outlines, sample test questions, answer sheets, and recommended study materials. Review of these materials is an essential part of test preparation. Candidates must learn beforehand the details of test administration. For example, knowing where the test will be given, the starting time, and transportation requirements are details whose consideration must not be delayed until the day before the test. Other requirements, such as admission tickets, identification, pencils, or permissible aids (calculators, drawing instruments), should be determined. What seems an obvious preparation can be most unsettling to a candidate if it is postponed until the hour before the test. Failure to attend to these types of details can greatly affect an individual's attitude and can result in poor performance.

When taking occupational tests, candidates should be instructed to answer all the questions. If they are uncertain about some questions, they should mark these questions so that they can review them if time permits. Most occupational tests are scored on the number of questions that are answered correctly, and there is no penalty for incorrect answers. Therefore, in taking occupational tests, guessing is recommended.

Some multiple-choice test-taking guides advise candidates either to choose or to avoid some choices or patterns of choices. It is this writer's experience that candidates are ill advised to follow any strategy based on the assumption that any particular pattern of choices will or will not appear on a test.

Occupational tests are more likely to be criterion-referenced than norm-referenced. The purpose of a criterion-referenced test is to reveal what a candidate knows or can do in a clearly defined domain of tasks. Responses on this type of test are scored solely on the basis of their ability to measure knowledge and skills in terms of specifically defined performance. The standard or cutscore (number of correct answers required) is set to represent the score that a minimally qualified candidate is expected to achieve.

Norm-referenced tests, in contrast, are designed to produce comparisons among candidates. Their purpose is to compare a student's performance (test score) with the performance of a clearly defined group (norm group) of other students. Scores are reported in percentile ranks, stanines, and grade equivalents. Questions are selected for these tests on the basis of their ability to "spread out" students on the score range. The measurement domain is broader for norm-referenced tests and includes such domains as reading ability, spelling, and addition (Thorndike, 1971). Vocational educators must prepare students to meet the prescribed standards of a criterion-referenced test and not to be concerned about how they compare to other students. The task domains for licensing and certification tests are generally made available to educators and should provide the basis for training programs.

References

California Department of Consumer Affairs. *What a Licensing Board Member Needs to Know About Consumer Affairs.* Sacramento, Calif.: Central Testing Unit, California Department of Consumer Affairs, 1983.

Fortune, J. C., and Associates. *Understanding Testing in Occupational Licensing.* San Francisco: Jossey-Bass, 1985.

Gellhorn, W. "The Abuse of Occupational Licensing." *The University of Chicago Law Review,* 1976, *44* (11), 6-27.

Grimm, K. L. "The Relationship of Accreditation to Voluntary Certification and State Licensure." In *Accreditation of Health Educational Programs: Part II—Staff Working Papers.* Washington, D.C.: National Commission on Accreditation, 1972.

Pellaton, J. "Does It Help to Prepare for a Licensure or Certification Test? Yes, Indeed." *COPASCOPE,* 1980, *2* (1), 1-2.

Rayack, E. *An Economic Analysis of Occupational Licensure.* Washington, D.C.: Manpower Administration, United States Department of Labor, 1976.

Shimberg, B. "Testing for Licensure and Certification." *American Psychologist,* 1981, *36* (10), 1138-1146.

Shimberg, B. *Occupational Licensing: A Public Perspective.* Princeton, N.J.: Educational Testing Service, 1982.

Shimberg, B. "The Relationship Among Accreditation, Certification and Licensure." Speech at the annual meeting of the Federation of State Medical Boards/77th annual congress on medical education, Chicago, April 7, 1984.

Thorndike, R. L. *Educational Measurement.* (2nd ed.) Washington, D.C.: American Council on Education, 1971.

U.S. Department of Health, Education and Welfare. *Report on Licensure and Related Health Personnel Credentialing.* DHEW publication 72-11. Washington, D.C.: U.S. Department of Health, Education and Welfare, 1971.

Charles J. Teryek is a program director at Educational Testing Service, Princeton, New Jersey. He is responsible for the development and management of licensing and certification programs in the health field.

This chapter presents essential concepts, strategies, and recommendations for implementing vertical articulation between occupational programs at high schools and two-year colleges.

Articulating Secondary and Postsecondary Occupational Programs

Joseph P. Arnold

Articulation is defined as an organized plan to assist students in making a smooth transition from one educational level to another. The purpose of this chapter is to present essential concepts, strategies, and recommendations for developing and implementing an articulation plan designed to help high school occupational graduates move successfully, and with minimal duplication of effort and few delays, into community colleges and other postsecondary occupational programs. Readers may wish to modify suggestions.

High school occupational students traditionally are prepared to go directly to work after high school, a decision normally made or assumed before they entered their vocational programs in the eleventh grade. They generally have not been considered "college material"; the main focus of college recruiters and high school counselors was on the college preparatory and upper ranks of the general-program students in the comprehensive high schools.

Many high school occupational program graduates possess two key ingredients to success in a postsecondary occupational program: favorable orientation to work and a career, and a well-developed interest and a background of skills and knowledge in an occupation or technology offered by the community colleges. Providing these students with awareness and encouragement, and directly assisting them in enrolling in community and technical college occupational programs, should be the mutual concern of high schools and colleges.

The Ohio Department of Education (Sterling, 1986) reports that Ohio high schools enrolled 279,397 eleventh and twelfth graders in 1985-86. Over 38 percent, or 106,730 of these students, were enrolled in vocational wage-earning programs throughout the state. Few people would contest the opinion that a substantial percentage of these 106,730 young people can benefit from the occupational program offerings of the community and technical colleges. Although high school vocational education nationally attracts a smaller percentage (27 percent) of high school students, the high school occupational programs may be the last largely untapped population of potential students for the community college.

Benefits of Articulation

Articulation between high school occupational education programs and the community and technical colleges has many benefits, both for students and for institutions. Petry (1978), the (Ohio) Joint Commission on Vocational and Technical Education (1983), and others describe the benefits and expectations of articulation. It appears that articulation:
- Arrests or eliminates duplication of effort in relation to courses and programs through arrangements for transfer credit for high school vocational students moving into community college and technical college programs
- Improves vocational and technical education program content and performance standards (at both high school and postsecondary levels)
- Promotes communication and cooperation among the state educational systems and among local institutions
- Promotes sharing of existing facilities and equipment
- Provides savings both for students and for articulating institutions.

Potential economic improvement, increased self-esteem, and personal satisfaction resulting from a higher level of student achievement should perhaps be regarded as the most important reasons for directing special effort toward articulation.

Types of Articulation

The idea of articulation between secondary schools and colleges has been with us for years but has become a priority since the late 1970s.

Long and others (1986) report only a minority of the articulation programs at seventy-two nationally selected sites as operational; most expect to start in 1985-86. Several types of articulation programs exist.

1. *Advanced placement* or *advanced standing programs* save time for high school occupational graduates by awarding credit for introductory college courses that are essentially equivalent to proficiencies learned in high school. Equivalency judgments can be quite informal comparisons made jointly by the community college occupational teacher and his or her counterpart in the high school. However, many states, community colleges, and high schools are rewriting courses in competency-based formats to provide more valid comparisons for establishing course equivalency. This type of program articulation assumes no attempt to unify or coordinate the two programs (high school and associate degree) to fulfill a single occupational goal.

2. *Pretech* or *core programs* are designed to produce better-prepared high school graduates for entry into postsecondary technical training programs by giving secondary students a broad technological preparation or a core of skills and concepts. Students are not required to make an occupational choice in the eleventh grade. The high school student may take more advanced training in place of any introductory courses that were bypassed at college entry. This articulation of eleventh and twelfth grades with the thirteenth and fourteenth years is geared to producing a more capable associate-degree graduate. Variations of this program are usually referred to as 2 + 2 programs.

3. *The four-year, 2 + 2 tech prep/associate degree program* recommended by Parnell (1985) runs parallel with the traditional college prep/baccalaureate degree program. It combines with the pretech core of learning (mostly in the eleventh and twelfth grades) with math, science, communications, and technology to produce a broadly based master technician. This program is planned to attract high school students who otherwise would be in the general track, as well as those in the vocational track.

Typical Activities and Strategies

The following principles and recommendations are outlined to help college and school staff understand and organize for articulation intended to move the high school occupational program graduate into a community or technical college.

The formality of the agreements, committee operations, and reporting will certainly vary among schools and colleges. While attempts to "keep it simple" should prevail, the plan may become rather formalized, in view of the involvement of the many people and the kinds of activities that are deemed necessary. In regard to the following activities, planners are urged to (1) select only the most important, highest priorities to accomplish, (2) obtain commitment at all educational levels, (3) share relevant, existing policies and materials, and (4) plan for a genuine working partnership among all institutions.

1. *Designate an individual from each participating institution and district to be responsible for the articulation effort in that institution.* This arrangement tends to establish all institutions as equal in status, provides contact persons, and fixes responsibilities for the work of the committees. These individuals will provide leadership throughout the effort and will need the authority of their titles as academic dean, principal, director of guidance services, supervisor, which will be helpful in appointing committees and working with other community and educational leaders.

2. *Develop and communicate a state or systemwide policy on articulation between the high schools and the community and technical colleges.* Many state education agencies, state community college boards, and professional organizations have adopted strong policies on articulation, making implementation at the local level a natural step in local high schools and community colleges. Without a state policy, it may be difficult for schools and colleges to take the issue seriously enough to invest in the long-range efforts needed to make articulation a reality.

A state articulation policy, developed by the state department and state board of community colleges or other cooperating authorities, may provide consultative assistance by state staff, written guidelines, additional state funds, improved public acceptance, and assistance in ameliorating "turf" and separatism issues between educational levels.

3. *Develop the articulation plan for implementation between the community college and the high school(s).* Assessing the current status of articulation between the college and the high school district (Nasman, Weber, and Denison, 1981) could be helpful in developing the overall articulation plan. A steering committee composed of key administrators from both institutions and some faculty is recommended. Middle-level administrators and faculty, as members of the group, will be helpful in developing and evaluating the plan as well as participating in the ongoing communication and selling job with faculty in the articulating institutions. State agency staff and policies, outside consultants, and the experience of neighboring institutions may play meaningful roles in this committee's work. Periodic meetings with faculty are suggested to obtain faculty input and build support for the plan.

4. *Determine student eligibility standards for admission, program placement, and/or advanced standing in college programs.* Faculty of the college must be willing to accept advanced standing or a similar concept of awarding credit. This is unlikely to occur without careful communication of the rationale for the total articulation effort and involvement of college teachers in determining the conditions for advanced standing.

5. *Develop a joint curriculum review process.* A committee composed of instructional supervisors, department chairpersons, faculty, curriculum specialists, and steering committee members is recommended. This group should be charged with the responsibility for determining the conditions for awarding advanced standing, the competency-based or other strategy to be utilized in making course and program comparisons, and developing the step-by-step process and procedures for establishing equivalency of courses. Additional joint curriculum committees composed of faculty and department chairpersons from the institutions are needed to compare and evaluate the programs and courses for advanced standing consideration. If a pretech 2 + 2 program is being planned, these groups will be considering extensive revisions of both high school and college programs.

6. *Develop strategies and guides for advising and counseling high school students and graduates who apply to the community college or technical college.* All colleges have professional staff, policies, and procedures for advising and counseling students. Initial contact by college recruiters most often occurs when students are high school juniors or seniors. However, these activities must start earlier in high school, when the student is making decisions about the future, rather than upon the student's arrival at college. The high school student must know about potential opportunities at the community college so that high school course and program choices can be made with some awareness. High school counselors should be aware of the specific requirements for advanced standing and other provisions of the plan for their students in each occupational program. College recruitment and admissions staff, selected faculty members, and department chairpersons usually will be expected to communicate the opportunities of advanced standing in special programs for high school students, both at the high school and at the college. College admission policies, brochures, and student handbooks generally will need to be rewritten. Both institutions should include appropriate policy statements on advanced standing and other key elements in the articulation effort.

7. *Develop written articulation agreements.* A written articulation agreement between the institutions is perhaps the most important link in the entire plan. According to the Ohio Council on Vocational Education (1986), agreements usually consist of

- A statement of intent
- Names of the institutions
- Period the agreement will be in effect
- General areas of cooperation
- Specific courses for which credit will be granted
- Equivalent credits to be granted
- Procedures and time limitations for granting credit
- Responsibilities of parties involved.

Agreements may be a product of the steering committee and normally are signed by the superintendent of the high school district and the president of the participating community or technical college.

8. *Plan for joint staff and teacher assignments between the high school and the community college or technical college.* Joint or shared staffing between the two institutions is unlikely to exist currently between the college and high schools. Ongoing, joint committee assignments—the steering committee, curriculum review committees, and others—certainly are necessary. The careful planning and coordination of committee activities will heavily influence the articulation effort.

High school occupational teachers, administrators, and counselors who periodically teach courses at the community or technical college (as part-time instructors) should develop an improved respect for and perspective on what the college can do for high school occupational graduates. Community college occupational teachers and high school teachers should be encouraged to form an exchange in which each periodically teaches the other's classes.

9. *Provide shared advisory committee membership for similar occupational programs at the two institutional levels.* Shared committee membership is supported by Petry (1978), Doty (1985), and others. Reorganizing advisory committees would no doubt be viewed favorably by members, assuming the occupations or technologies of interest have high similarity. Schools and colleges expecting to move into a four-year 2 + 2 tech prep/associate degree program should give strong consideration to appointing a single unified advisory committee or merging existing committees serving highly similar programs in the high school and community or technical college programs.

10. *Plan and conduct orientation and training programs for staff of both institutions.* Orientation of the total school and college staffs need not be complex but is vital to gaining needed understanding and support as the articulation program is developed. Many faculty and instructional supervisors from both levels will need to be assigned to various roles in the program as implementation proceeds. Curriculum review (to establish the equivalence or similarity of programs and courses) and curriculum revision (to establish a pretech 2 + 2 program) are highly important activities in the articulation process. These assignments, therefore, deserve adequate time, a clearly defined charge of responsibility, and provision of appropriate training at the expense of the articulating institutions.

11. *Plan the sharing of facilities and equipment.* It should be nothing new for facilities and equipment to be shared in whatever manner may be desired by both institutions. Community colleges and high schools alike may occasionally need instructional laboratories, classrooms, or items of equipment that another institution may already have but may not be utilizing fully. Any sharing of this nature is likely to be helpful to one or

both institutions, but the real winners are the taxpayers, who otherwise would pay for an additional facility. This form of cooperation can be facilitated by articulation planning and obviously can be enormously beneficial to the public image of both institutions.

12. *Develop a joint annual budget for articulation activities.* Much of the direct expense of articulation planning can often be assumed by existing accounts. Some expenses may go well beyond the expected limitations, however. Training, consultants, staff travel, and publications are best budgeted early in the project. If some faculty and staff are expected to undergo training, it must be accomplished at the expense of an employing institution or of the articulation project. It is also possible that load reductions for a few faculty members may be necessary if pervasive curriculum revision is required.

Many institutions involved in articulation planning and operation claim no additional budget is necessary. However, if extra work is assigned to teachers, without load reduction or extra remuneration, very little or no articulation progress can be expected. Whatever funds are required should be considered as a worthwhile investment likely to show returns in many positive ways.

Closing Remarks

Articulation planning and implementation forces a pervasive review of nearly all school and college policies and procedures. Administrative roles and relationships with other institutions; guidance, admissions, and recruitment; teacher roles; curriculum design and review; faculty and staff development; the appointment and use of business and industry advisory committees: All may be seriously affected by articulation planning and implementation.

Joint planning and activities between colleges and high schools has to be beneficial for all parties. When institutional leaders, faculty, student service, and other personnel from two institutions meet regularly to accomplish common goals, suspicions, jealousies, and separatist attitudes must vanish. Sharing and open communication have to improve the mutual respect between institutional staffs and enhance the public images of all colleges and schools involved.

As for the direction and ambitions of the articulation effort, the first question to answer is "What type and how much articulation is needed in our particular institutions and by our students?" A time-shortened plan may be acceptable as a first phase, but the various 2 + 2 possibilities must be considered as we realize their potential benefits to students and society. Although many barriers may be encountered, the articulation process appears to be a definite breakthrough for helping occupational high school programs and community and technical colleges to accomplish goals neither has been able to accomplish previously on its own.

References

Doty, C. R. "Vertical Articulation of Occupational Education from Secondary Schools to Community Colleges." *Journal of Technical Careers*, 1985, 7 (2), 98-112. (ED 272 673)

Joint Commission on Vocational and Technical Education. *Improving the Partnership*. Columbus: Ohio Board of Regents and the State Board of Education, 1983.

Long, J. P., and others. *Avenues for Articulation: Coordinating Secondary and Postsecondary Programs*. Columbus: National Center for Research in Vocational Education, The Ohio State University, 1986. (ED 264 445)

Nasman, L. O., Weber, J. M., and Denison, R. H. *The Cuyahoga Community College/Cleveland Public Schools Articulation Assessment Constituent Survey Report*. Columbus: National Center for Research in Vocational Education, Ohio State University, 1981.

Ohio Council on Vocational Education. *High School Vocational Programs/Two Year College Technical Programs: In the Articulation Spotlight*. Columbus: Ohio Council on Vocational Education, 1986.

Parnell, D. *The Neglected Majority*. Washington, D.C.: The Community College Press, 1985.

Petry, J. P. *Tennessee Vocational Education Articulation Project: Final Report*. Memphis, Tenn.: Bureau of Educational Research and Services, 1978. (ED 170 575)

Sterling, G. *Annual Job Training Secondary Enrollment Report, 1985-86*. Columbus: Research, Survey, Evaluation, and Exemplary Programs, Division of Vocational and Career Education, Ohio Department of Education, 1986.

Joseph P. Arnold is professor of education and director of the Office of Two-Year College Professional Development, University of Akron. He was formerly a technical college academic dean and an Ohio Board of Regents staff administrator.

This chapter contains major questions on structuring curricula as well as program sources, and suggests actions.

General Education in the Occupational Curriculum: Why? To What Extent? With What Results?

Dale F. Campbell, Mary T. Wood

Support for general education in the occupational curriculum has waxed and waned over the history of the community college movement. Current leaders in this field appear to be in greater agreement that general education is a viable component of the associate degree program and that it is the component that provides the primary avenue through which students achieve the desired abilities to think, reason, compute, communicate, and adapt to change.

The major question in this educational era appears to be not whether to incorporate general education into the occupational curriculum, but to what degree it should be included, by what method it should be incorporated, and by what technique its results can be judged. In recent years national educational organizations such as the American Association of Community and Junior Colleges and the National Council for Occupational Education have expressed renewed interest in and commitment to general education in the community college curriculum.

States are requiring general education and its role in the community college curriculum to be evaluated. Therefore, it is essential for practitioners to examine the various perspectives related to the philosophical and conceptual basis for strengthening general education, as well as the issues and problems of implementing a stronger general education component in the community college occupational curriculum.

Renewed Emphasis on General Education

In the late sixties and seventies in most community colleges across the nation, emphasis was placed on building the occupational programs. Research reveals that enrollment in occupational programs in two-year colleges in the United States increased from 40 percent of total enrollment during the 1960s (Bushnell, 1973) to over 50 percent of total enrollment during the 1970s (Parker, 1974).

This period of rapid growth in these programs occurred in many cases without time or effort devoted to strong curriculum design and evaluation. General education components in many programs were weak. As the growth of occupational programs stabilized in the early eighties (Mahoney, 1985), many educators took a closer look at curriculum programs. Support and interest emerged for stronger, more accountable curriculum design (Justin, 1985).

During this review period, a renewed emphasis on the general education component of occupational programs emerged. The move to identify competencies needed by program graduates led to increased interaction between the colleges and businesses and industries, particularly in the occupational programs of the community colleges (Halyard and Murphy, 1978).

The outcome identification process involving personnel of colleges, businesses, and industries revealed a strong desire for community college graduates to possess skills in reading, writing, thinking, analyzing, and adapting. Authors of community college literature expressed concern for "merger of career and liberal education," recognizing that "both are part of a functioning person" (Sagen, 1979). Many writers echoed the sentiments of Harris and Grede (1977) with a "call to integrate the practical and liberal to prepare students for careers, not jobs."

National organizations concerned with community college education expressed renewed concern about general education components in occupational curricula. The American Association of Community and Junior Colleges (AACJC) expressed support for the inclusion of a strong general education component in its Policy Statement on the Associate Degree, adopted by the AACJC board of directors in 1984. This document states in part, "All degree programs should reflect those characteristics that help define what constitutes an educated person. Such characteristics include a level of general education that enables the individual to understand and appreciate his or her culture and environment, the development of a system of personal values based on accepted ethics that lead to civic and social responsibility, and the attainment of skills in analysis, communication, quantification, and synthesis necessary for further growth as a lifespan learner and a productive member of society."

The National Council for Occupational Education also committed strong support for the general education component in its policy statement, prepared in 1985 by the Task Force on the Associate in Applied Science Degree. This statement reveals "an increased recognition of the importance of general education and related studies as integral components of occupational education. Increasingly, the ability to think, reason, compute, communicate, and adapt to change are essential if workers at all levels are to remain employable and cope with the expanding knowledge base."

Supporting these educational organizations, national accrediting agencies are addressing the need for stronger emphasis on general education in higher education curriculum programs. In their recent article reviewing standards related to the general education component in the associate degree program, Porter and Bender (1985) support the requirement for a general education standard for the associate degree and outline the standards adopted for the general education component of the associate degree programs by the Commission on Colleges.

In 1984, the Commission on Colleges, Southern Association of Colleges and Schools, adopted criteria for accreditation, placing major emphasis on general education. These criteria require that the general education or liberal arts component constitute a minimum of 25 percent of the total number of hours required for degree completion at the postsecondary level. In 1985, the Executive Council of the Commission on Colleges adopted a proposed reworking of the standards to incorporate guidelines stating that for degree completion in associate programs, the general education component must constitute a minimum of fifteen semester hours or the equivalent and must be drawn from humanities or fine arts, the social or behavioral sciences, and the natural sciences or mathematics.

In addition to the support for general education provided by accrediting agencies, and to legislation requiring the general education curriculum be evaluated, there are now requirements in some states that tests such as the College Level Academic Skills Test (CLAST), first given in Florida in 1982 for two-year college students, be employed to judge student achievement. These factors, in combination with the increasing demands of a highly technological society for a citizenry that can think, read, compute, adjust, change, adapt, and cope, prompt a serious review of the role of general education in the occupational curricula of community colleges.

Issues in the Merger of General Education and Occupational Education

Making a strong plea for "liberal education for the informed citizen," Cohen and Brawer (1982, p. 328) maintain that community colleges must "provide some portion of the education for the masses that tends toward encouraging exercise of the intellect." If community college educators are indeed beginning to agree that general education is a viable component of occupational curricula—a necessary part of the associate degree, and the major avenue for students' acquisition of necessary life skills—then what barriers prevent the smooth implementation of successful, integrated curriculum programs?

Content is a major issue in the integration of general education into occupational curricula. To date, many curriculum guides have outlined the general education component in terms of courses and credit hours in communications, behavioral or social sciences, and humanities. In many cases, colleges have simply added to the occupational programs traditional courses from the general education or transfer curriculum. In most cases these courses have not met the needs of the occupational programs.

The competency-based education movement, which has had a major impact on many occupational programs in recent years, has forced curriculum developers to seriously address the identification on specific skills necessary for each occupational program. The general education component in these programs has proved a difficult arena in which to complete this type of skill-identification process. In most cases, program developers agree that reading, writing, thinking, analysis, and adaptation skills need to be taught, but often these skills are still vaguely defined and remain difficult to measure. Specific general education courses designed to teach these skills to occupational students have not been developed. Evaluation methods and programs for measuring attainment of general education skills are still weak, and mastery in most cases is still determined by successful course completion.

Another issue that must be addressed is the lack of coordinated effort between the general education and occupational faculties in defining outcomes and developing courses. Administrative commitment, educational leadership, and perseverance are required to support faculty integration in a successful movement to implement a strong general education component in occupational programs. Many attempts have all but failed because of the difficulty of the task (O'Banion and Shaw, 1982).

The desire to meet the general education needs of both the degree completer and the degree continuer in one selected program of general education is another issue to be addressed by curriculum designers in the two-year curricula. If the student who plans to go on to a four-year institution still needs introductory-level courses, how does this need mesh with the terminal degree student's need for broad integrated courses in particular content areas?

Campbell and Korim (1979), in their review of occupational programs in four-year colleges, address several of the issues faced by curriculum planners in designing occupational programs to meet the needs of the institution as well as the needs of students. Among the most pervasive issues are the substantial differences between occupational education curricula and 2 + 2 curricula, and disagreement over the extent to which articulation with vocational schools and secondary vocational programs is desirable (Campbell and Korim, 1979). This curriculum-development area requires careful study from two-year curriculum developers and stronger efforts toward articulation with senior institutions.

Barriers to Successful Merger

General education in the community college has been charged with a large task, and meeting the life-skills needs of the occupational student has become a major component of this charge. In order to meet national organization demands, state legislative mandates, and student needs for general education in the occupational curricula, several problems must be addressed.

The definition of general education embodies a major barrier to successful program integration. In its sixty-year history, innumerable definitions of general education have been used, ranging from the narrow to the broad. It has been defined as the vehicle for providing the basic understandings and skills that all citizens should possess and has been charged with the responsibility of meeting Jefferson's ideal of enlightening people so that they can function in a democracy. Cohen and Brawer (1982) note that the vagueness of the definition of general education is a major widespread difficulty in successful implementation of general educational efforts into the community college.

The loose structure of the total general education curriculum poses a second barrier to successful implementation. Most general education efforts are strongly departmentalized, with little training of faculty in the development of interdisciplinary courses. In addressing the general education needs of occupational programs, there is a lack of shared understanding between the general education faculty and occupational faculty of the students' needs in both of these areas of the curriculum. Most general education faculty tend to develop introductory courses in their particular disciplines and incorporate these offerings into the occupational curriculum without regard for the unique general education needs of the occupational student.

Traditions established during the early community college movement pose a third barrier. In most cases, integration of general education into occupational programs was left to individual community colleges, and each college "did its own thing." These early efforts lacked strong state or federal leadership in philosophy and curriculum design.

The increased demand for community colleges to address declining literacy in the United States has created another barrier for implementing general education into occupational programs. The need to add basic skills training, developmental programs, and remedial courses to the community college curriculum has created an additional area of concern. Compensatory education efforts have increased the time and effort expended by most students in occupational education programs. Yet, regardless of how general education is defined or addressed in the occupational curriculum, mastery of basic skills in reading, writing, computing, and studying is required (Roueche and Roueche, 1982).

New Approaches

In attempts to overcome these barriers, many colleges have undertaken innovative approaches. These approaches include coordinated efforts by general education and occupational education faculty to develop integrated courses designed specifically for occupational students, and new approaches to the evaluation of general education in the occupational curriculum.

Perhaps the most widely recognized program of reform in general education is at Miami-Dade Community College. In a project begun in 1975, the college inaugurated a program of institutional reform to improve academic standards in general education.

Using a comprehensive approach, the college first reviewed and revised general education requirements, building on areas of the general education curriculum that had proved most successful in the past. Second, the college built a general education program with four major components: a rationale, goals, courses and objectives for attaining the goals, and evaluation. This process provided a basis for a clearer understanding of the need and reasons for general education. It also established general education goals to guide students in setting their own. One important aspect of goal setting in this process involved agreement among the majority of faculty and administrators about general education goals. Third, the college developed a strong general education program that provided the core for the entire community college curriculum. General education goals applied to most degree-seeking students. The changes brought about by this process of curriculum development required strong administrative leadership and support to ensure that faculty participation, and the support necessary to effect the desired change in general education offerings, were present.

The general education program at Miami-Dade Community College incorporates a strong developmental studies component. The responsibility for the development of students' skills in reading and writing is shared by a cross-section of the faculty.

A unique feature of Miami-Dade's general education program is incorporation of the program into the college's student flow model. This model provides a structure to ensure that students can move systematically from enrollment to their degree of choice.

The Miami-Dade general education program includes five courses: one in communications, one in the humanities, "The Individual," "The Social Environment," and "The National Environment." These courses, required of all degree-seeking students, are designed specifically to meet the general education goals of the college. Other courses from the general education program may also be required, depending on the student's chosen curriculum.

In support of its general education effort, Miami-Dade has also developed a network of student support systems to aid students in completing degree requirements. These systems of student support include a set of academic standards, an "academic alert" system, and the Advisement and Graduation Information System (AGIS). The use of these student support systems enables the college to provide special assistance to students and to help them complete the general education program as well as the other degree requirements.

The Miami-Dade program is one attempt to meet the unique needs of community college students, to maintain the open-door system, and to provide both the general education and the occupational skills necessary for students to participate successfully in today's society (Lukenbill and McCabe, 1982).

Through the guidance and financial assistance provided by the National Endowment for the Humanities, several community colleges have made progress in improving the humanities components of their occupational curricula. James Sprunt Community College, a small rural community college in eastern North Carolina, is one such institution. In a five-year period beginning in 1978, the college developed a comprehensive plan for humanities education through revision and expansion of its humanities offerings in the vocational and technical curricula. A cooperative effort between the general education faculty and the occupational faculty made instruction in the humanities available to every occupational program at the college. The plan was based on an institutional philosophy that stresses the teaching of the humanities to all students, regardless of their chosen fields of study or career interests. Although the primary mission of the college is to provide occupation training, the administration and the faculty are committed to the concept of "total education," of which the humanities are considered an integral part. The college offers three interdisciplinary humanities courses for technical students: "The Nature of Man," "The Nature of America," and "The Future of Man." In addition to one of the three humanities courses, two English courses are required of all two-year degree-seeking students in occupational programs. Additional humanities courses, entitled "Southern Culture," "The Black Experience," "Politics, Economics, and Human Affairs," and "Society and the Individual" (Fife, 1980), and a humanistically oriented social science course, are available as electives for two-year occupational students. A humanities course, available for all one-year diploma students, includes five units of study: culture and society, the social order, politics, economics, and the individual (Rowe, 1984).

As a result of the emphasis on curriculum revision, students seeking the two-year associate degree in general education meet the following core requirements: two English composition courses, one fine-arts or philosophy course, two social science courses, two humanities courses, one mathematics course, and one science course. These curriculum revisions have introduced a strong general education component into all occupational programs of the college. The addition of humanities has supported the college's philosophy that career education, in its broadest and best sense, should be a reasonable balance between preparation for earning a living and preparation for living (Fife, 1980).

Community colleges have used a variety of approaches to general education. Los Medanos College, in California, has incorporated a self-directed study requirement as a part of its general education program, in an attempt to help students become more self-directive and responsible (Collins, 1978). Interdisciplinary courses based on common human experiences form the core of the general education program developed by Catonsville Community College, in Maryland. In addition to other general education credits, all graduates of this school's two-year associate degree programs have taken two humanities courses, "Exploration of Nature and Society" and "Exploration of Ideas and Images." At Kirkwood Community College, in Iowa, the general education curriculum is being reviewed and revised through a Central Disciplines program entitled "Strengthening Humanities Through Faculty Development." This is another program supported by the National Endowment for the Humanities.

Another curriculum reform movement in general education is being employed by the University of Kentucky. New requirements for freshmen entering in the fall of 1988 were approved in 1986. The new general education plan will stress writing skills in all general education courses and require students to complete two courses that integrate knowledge in different academic fields. Students are also required to take a cross-cultural course that addresses a Third World or non-Western civilization.

These curriculum reforms have implications for the University of Kentucky's thirteen community colleges; the two-year institutions have to adjust their programs to prepare students who plan to transfer to earn bachelor's degrees. Similar actions have occurred at approximately 59 percent of the nation's four-year institutions in recent years.

Most faculty members agree that several factors have influenced the nationwide general education reforms. These factors include a national call for more stringent educational standards, a renewed effort to define what it means to be educated, an effort to ensure that all students have basic skills, and a recognition of the need for instilling in students attitudes and values that promote an appreciation for lifelong learning (Jester, 1986).

The Future: Suggestions for Action

The following suggestions may prove helpful to occupational education leaders:

1. Development of a strong institutional philosophy and an accompanying commitment to general education in the occupational curriculum is the cornerstone of a successful effort. Knowledgeable and committed leadership is imperative.

2. Training for administrators and faculty must be provided to ensure a coordinated effort by the general education and occupation programs.

3. A coordinated general education and occupational faculty effort to address the competencies needed for successful living is essential.

4. These coordinated efforts should extend to developing integrated courses designed specifically to meet the identified needs of students in occupational programs.

5. Institutions should develop and implement strong evaluation processes to measure individual course and comprehensive outcomes. Follow-up evaluation programs on graduates should be developed and regularly employed.

6. As states move toward legislative mandates for program accountability in general education, colleges should work cooperatively and provide leadership in setting guidelines for general education components.

7. Community colleges should continue articulation efforts with four-year colleges. Addressing the general education needs of two-year graduates and transfer students remains an important consideration for program developers.

8. The community college must reexamine the two-year time frame for the occupational degree in light of students' needs, general education demands, and increased occupational needs due to advancing technology.

If community college educators take seriously the need for general education in occupational curricula, there must be no retreat from the challenge of ensuring that each student learns what he or she needs to know not only to survive but also to thrive in today's society and to prepare for the future.

Program Contacts

Drew Rowe, Director, General Education
James Sprunt Community College
P.O. Box 398
Kenansville, NC 28349

Rhonda Kekke, Director of NEH Grant
Kirkwood Community College
6301 Kirkwood Blvd. SW
Cedar Rapids, IA 52406

Ray Quigley
Catonsville Community College
800 S. Rolling Road
Baltimore Ct., MD 21228

References

American Association of Community and Junior Colleges. "Policy Statement on The Associate Degree." Adopted by the AACJC Board of Directors, July 7, 1984.

Bushnell, D. S. *Organizing for Change: New Priorities for Community Colleges.* New York: McGraw-Hill, 1973.

Campbell, D. F., and Korim, A. S. *Occupational Programs in Four-Year Colleges: Trends and Issues.* ERIC/Higher Education Research Report no. 5. Washington, D.C.: American Association for Higher Education, 1979. (ED 176 645)

Cohen, A. M., and Brawer, F. *The American Community College.* San Francisco: Jossey-Bass, 1982. (ED 213 469)

Collins, C. C. "General Education at Los Medanos College: A Curricular Model." Paper presented at the Danforth Foundation Conference on General and Liberal Education, St. Louis, March 16-18, 1978.

Fife, T. *Humanities for Technical Students.* Kenansville, N.C.: James Sprunt Technical College, 1980.

Halyard, R. A., and Murphy, N. "Using Competency-Based Techniques in Curriculum Development." Papers presented at the 58th annual convention of the American Association of Community and Junior Colleges, Atlanta, Ga., April 9-12, 1978. (ED 154 868)

Harris, N. C., and Grede, J. F. *Career Education in Colleges: A Guide for Planning Two- and Four-Year Occupational Programs.* San Francisco: Jossey-Bass, 1977.

Jester, A. "UK Announces Tougher Degree Requirements." *Lexington Herald-Leader,* February 16, 1986, Section B, p. 1.

Justin, M. J. "Involvement in Learning: The Three Keys." *Community and Junior College Journal,* 1985, 55 (7), 23-28.

Lukenbill, J. D., and McCabe, R. H. "Getting Started: Straightforward Advice." In B. Lamar Johnson (ed.), *General Education in Two-Year Colleges.* New Directions for Community Colleges, no. 40. San Francisco: Jossey-Bass, 1982. (ED 222 236)

Mahoney, James R. (ed.). *1985 Community Technical and Junior College Directors.* Washington, D.C.: American Association of Community and Junior Colleges, 1985.

O'Banion, T., and Shaw, R. G. "Obstacles to General Education." In B. Lamar Johnson (ed.), *General Education in Two-Year Colleges.* New Directions for Community Colleges, no. 40. San Francisco: Jossey-Bass, 1982. (ED 222 236)

Parker, G. G. *Career Education and Transfer Program Enrollment in Two-Year Colleges, 1973-74.* ACT Special Report no. 11. Iowa City: American College Testing Program, 1974. (ED 103 031)

Porter, G. H., and Bender, L. W. "General Education and the Associate Degree." *Proceedings,* 1985, 38 (1), 2-4.

Roueche, S. D., and Roueche, J. E. "Literacy Development: Foundation for General Education." In B. Lamar Johnson (ed.), *General Education in Two-Year Colleges.* New Directions for Community Colleges, no. 40. San Francisco: Jossey-Bass, 1982. (ED 222 236)

Rowe, F. A., Jr. *Learning for Living.* Kenansville, N.C.: James Sprunt Technical College, 1984.

Sagen, H. B. "Careers, Competencies, and Liberal Education." Paper presented at annual meeting of the Association of American Colleges, Washington, D.C., February 1979. (ED 179 185)

Task Force on the Associate in Applied Science Degree. *Criteria for Excellence in Associate in Applied Science Degree Programs.* A policy statement of the National Council for Occupational Education. El Paso, Tex.: El Paso Community College District, 1985.

Dale F. Campbell is assistant commissioner for Community Colleges and Technical Institutes, Texas State College and University System Coordinating Board.

Mary T. Wood is an education administrator at James Sprunt Community College, Kenansville, N.C.

This chapter presents a pragmatic approach to occupational program evaluation at multicampus, single intermediate, and small-campus settings. The Dallas County Community College District evaluation process is used as a model.

Occupational Program Evaluation

Ted Martinez, Jr., Barbara S. Echord

Community colleges and technical institutes must meet a broad spectrum of educational needs and work-force demands. Consequently, they must systematically assess their programs' relevance and quality. Improvement of instruction, updating of programs, and efficient use of resources are the real purposes of occupational program evaluation.

At the Dallas County Community College District (DCCCD), occupational program evaluation is closely linked to the goals of the college and district as they relate to occupational education. It is DCCCD's policy to monitor technical and occupational training needs of the Dallas area, and to offer courses through one- and two-year programs that impart the skills and technical knowledge required for employment in semiprofessional and other occupational fields.

Occupational program evaluation is basically a campus activity. The occupational dean and the occupational education task force have primary roles in the entire process. In multicampus systems, a district staff can assist by providing coordination, support, and relevant data. On single campuses, a third party, such as a state agency, can be involved. In both cases, employers (advisory committee members) should be included in the evaluation process. Employers tend to be candid, to relate training programs to their businesses, and to be rather comfortable with evaluation (Paris, 1985).

Evaluation in a Multicampus Institution

DCCCD is composed of seven campuses serving approximately 90,000 students. About half these students are enrolled in credit programs and half in noncredit programs. DCCCD has approximately 25,000 occupational education students in over 100 one- and two-year occupational programs. As such numbers tend to suggest, program evaluation is not easy, but it is essential in a setting as large and complex as this. Thus, the college district has developed program evaluation procedures and a program evaluation planning cycle.

The function of DCCCD's District Office for Career and Continuing Education is to coordinate, market, and evaluate occupational continuing education programs for all campuses. An assistant director in this office at the district level monitors and coordinates the program evaluation that takes place at each campus. In addition, the district office also provides helpful data on costs, enrollment, and high school student interest.

With district staff providing this coordination and support, the occupational dean at each campus, working with the vice-president for instruction and the division chairperson for the selected programs, has primary responsibility for the evaluation of the programs at that campus. When similar programs are offered at two or three different campuses, each is evaluated in the same semester. The evaluations are all conducted separately, but coordination of information is provided by the district office.

Phase I: Data Collection. DCCCD's evaluation plan sets forth a three-phase process. In phase I, the occupational dean begins by meeting with appropriate staff at the campus to identify and schedule the programs to be evaluated. When the schedule is completed, the district office, the occupational dean, and the vice-president for instruction appoint an occupational education task force and assign responsibilities. Task force members represent the campus and include the occupational dean, the continuing education dean, occupational and liberal arts faculty, the division chair, and a business office representative. Program advisory committee members are also invited, as appropriate. The task force begins an intensive data-collection process, with individual action plans designed to ensure accountability.

The collected data become the basis for an occupational program profile compiled by the occupational dean. The profile configures data around four categories: capability, funding, importance of program, and market viability, as follows:

- *Capability* includes information on instructional factors, instructional personnel, facilities, and equipment. The instructional factors include data on curriculum analysis, program completers, performance, costs, and the like. The intention is to determine the ability of a program to provide appropriate instruction.

- *Funding* includes student statistics, cost per contact hour, and comparison data with other programs at DCCCD.
- *Importance* includes data on how relevant a program is to the campus and to the district.
- *Market viability* includes employment-demand data from the state's 1202 Commission, the Texas Employment Commission, the U.S. Department of Labor, and local employer questionnaires, as well as input from the semiannual meetings of the program advisory committee. Student-interest data collected by the district are also included. These data come from surveys of local Explorer Scouts and intermediate school district students.

Phase II: Program Analysis. Phase II involves occupational program analysis (Figure 1). In essence, it is a modification of what is known as portfolio analysis in business. This phase depends on the data that have been compiled by the task force through the program profiles. Those data are "plugged in" to the analysis process as it addresses a service area through consideration of the student, general, and business communities. The task force uses the data to reach consensus (or majority) in each area.

Basically, programs offered at a specific campus should deliver up-to-date instruction. Each campus serves a designated sector of the county. Thus, the questions the program analysis asks concern such external factors as the service area involved, the types of incoming students, and the needs of the general community. Under the topic *general community* are considered such questions as "To what extent is DCCCD the only provider in Dallas County? If we discontinue the program at this campus, will there be a negative reaction?" For example, one campus, Brookhaven College, recently attempted to discontinue a child development lab, but an outcry from the community convinced Brookhaven to retain the program. Because service areas for each DCCCD campus are very different, each campus is asked to examine instructional services to business and industry, involvement with business and industry, high-tech emphasis, and entrepreneurship. The program analysis uses districtwide weighted scores in the student and general community columns. Each campus determines the weighted score for its service area with respect to the business community.

The task force then invites the division chair and the program faculty to participate in the analysis. The task force assigns a ranking, with 1 as low and 5 as high. Ranking multiplied by weighted scores yields total score for each program. This process helps in setting priorities for local programs, in descending order (Figure 2). Programs are then designated as having high, medium, or low priority.

Phase III: Cross-Comparisons of Programs. In phase III, the task force uses a series of matrices (Figure 3) to compare external factors to the internal factors of capability, funding, importance, and market viability. The task force must reach consensus on the relative capability, funding,

Figure 1. Application of Criteria to Programs and Services

College: _____

Criteria (0-5, with 5=Highest)

PROGRAM/SERVICE	STUDENT					GENERAL COMMUNITY								(Max. 8) BUSINESS COMMUNITY						Total Score
	Program (4) Provides Current Knowledge		Job Demand (5)			Program Meets (4) Perceived Training Needs of Community		To What (2) Extent is the DCCCD the Only Provider		Severe Negative (2) Reaction Will Follow if Abandoned or Ignored		Instructional Services to Bus/Ind. ( )		Involvement w/ Bus/Ind. ( )		Hi-Tech Emphasis ( )		Entrepreneurship ( )		
	Ct.	Score	Ct.	Score		Ct.	Score	Ct.	Score	Ct.	Score	Ct.	Score	Ct.	Score	Ct.	Score	Ct.	Score	

Ct. (Criteria) x (x) (Weight) = Score

Figure 2. Ranked Inventory of Programs and Services

College: _____

PROGRAM/SERVICES IN DESCENDING ORDER	SCORE	SERVICE AREA PRIORITIES		
		HIGH	MEDIUM	LOW

PROGRAM/SERVICES

1
2
3
4
5
6
7
8
9
10
11
12
13

Figure 3. Cross-Comparison Matrices

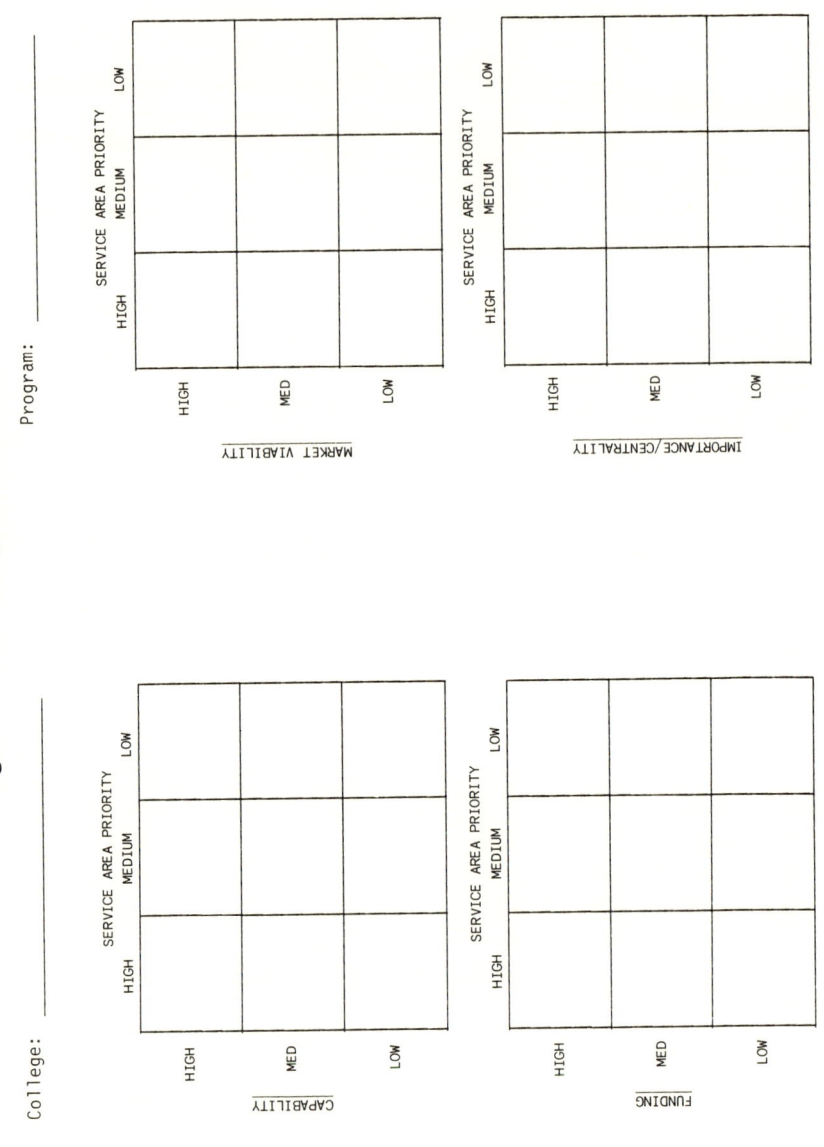

College: _____   Program: _____

importance, centrality, and market viability for each program by assigning a high, medium, or low rating. This is not an easy task. A program may be able to provide excellent, up-to-date instruction, but local need for the program may be very low.

Finally, the task force makes recommendations about improving, maintaining, or relaxing one or all of the internal factors. These recommendations are forwarded to the vice-president for instruction and to the president.

Districtwide Summative Evaluation. At the conclusion of this process, program profiles will have been completed for all programs in the system. Each program at each campus will be ranked according to its score. On the basis of these analyses, the campus administration will make decisions about how to proceed with each program—by cutting back or enhancing funding, increasing marketability, and so forth. Finally, with the program information from each of the campuses, the District Office will develop a districtwide summary of all DCCCD occupational education programs.

Naturally, this evaluation process has a few snags. For example, when the process was initiated, persons assigned to occupational education task forces were somewhat intimidated by the program profile used to guide data collection. As they became more involved, this complexity began to excite them. The profiles increased their work effectiveness by helping them examine programs critically but fairly.

Another concern was that some programs seemed inevitably to end up at the bottom in the rankings, but even in these cases the faculty generally already knew how their programs were weak and how they would rank. It is true that a program may be phased out through this process. DCCCD has emphasized, however, that even when rankings are low, the evaluation process can be seen as positive—that is, the evaluation may reveal that a program can be strengthened, rather than eliminated. It may suggest that funding should be increased, outdated equipment replaced, marketing boosted, and so forth. The evaluation process can help in developing strategies to improve programs' rankings.

Evaluation in a Single Intermediate or Small Institution

Although the program evaluation model is designed for a large multicampus district, this model may be applicable to single intermediate or small-campus settings. When it is impossible to evaluate all programs annually, an evaluation schedule is used to review a percentage of the programs each semester. Figure 4 shows a three-year rotation cycle for evaluating occupational programs. In establishing a rotation cycle, it is important to consider programs that require annual evaluation, such as

Figure 4. Three-Year Rotation Cycle for Evaluating Occupational Programs

FALL SEMESTER 1986	SPRING SEMESTER 1987	FALL SEMESTER 1987	FALL SEMESTER 1988
Drafting	Electronics	Welding	Electronics
Word Processing	Auto Body	Word Processing	Marketing
Child Development	Ornamental Horticulture	Commercial Music	Graphic Arts
Computer Technology	Criminal Justice	Computer Technology	Foods Technology
Automotive Technology	Mental Health	Management	Legal Assistant

FALL SEMESTER 1988	SPRING SEMESTER 1989	FALL SEMESTER 1989	SPRING SEMESTER 1990
Real Estate	Animal Medical	Drafting	Electronics
Word Processing	Hospitality Management	Word Processing	Auto Body
Machine Shop	Horology	Child Development	Ornamental Horticulture
Computer Technology	Interior Design	Computer Technology	Criminal Justice
Fire Protection	Human Services	Automotive Technology	Mental Health

new programs or programs whose economic and technological factors drive curriculum or funding.

It is important that the college appoint a staff administrator to coordinate the evaluation process, assist instructional areas as programs are reviewed, serve as central "clearinghouse" in the dissemination of materials, and to assist the instructional dean in the preparation of summary reports.

On single intermediate or small campuses, the responsibilities of the occupational dean in the previously discussed model should be assumed by the instructional dean. In phase I, the instructional dean meets with staff at the college to identify and schedule the programs to be evaluated and to appoint the occupational education task forces. The chair of each task force is a representative from a department that is not evaluated during that cycle.

The staff administrator is responsible for providing the task force with information on instructional factors, program funding, and market viability. The collected data become the basis of the profile compiled by the task force. The task force uses the data from the profile to begin phase II of the program analysis: examining the community college service area, the data on incoming students, and the needs of the general community.

The task force, division chair, and program faculty, using Figure 1, rate the program according to the criteria already mentioned. To obtain the final score, each rating is multiplied by the weighted score and summed.

As in the DCCCD model, the task force completes phase III, using Figure 3 to compare service-area priorities to capability, funding, importance, and market viability (internal factors) of programs. In its report to the instructional dean, the task force makes recommendations on improving, maintaining, or relaxing one or all of the internal factors.

The instructional dean reviews and compares the data and recommendations from all occupational programs for all phases and submits a report to the president or to the administrative council.

If an evaluation schedule is used, program profiles and recommendations for programs evaluated every three years are reviewed by the instructional dean before the final report is submitted.

Monitoring and assessing technical and occupational programs is a responsibility community colleges must continue to assume in order to meet work-force demands, update instruction, coordinate program resources, and determine priorities for program spending. A systematic model for evaluating technical and occupational programs provides the analysis administrators need in determining the future status of these programs at the campus and district levels.

Reference

Paris, K. A. "Employers as Evaluators." *Community, Technical, and Junior College Journal*, 1985, 55 (6), 28-30.

Ted Martinez, Jr., is district director of career and continuing education at Dallas County Community College District.

Barbara S. Echord is assistant district director of career and continuing education at Dallas County Community College District.

This chapter provides an annotated bibliography of relevant materials made available through the Educational Resources Information Center (ERIC).

Sources and Information: Occupational Program Development at the Postsecondary Level

Charles R. Doty, Mary P. Hardy

An annotated bibliography of recent ERIC documents dealing with occupational curriculum development is presented in this concluding chapter. Also included are materials about organizations and associations serving as resources for up-to-date curriculum information.

The documents included in the bibliography were selected from additions to the ERIC data base since 1980, with priority given to practitioner-oriented materials. Although many of the documents were not produced by or exclusively for community, junior, and technical colleges, most of the material can be applied to the two-year college setting. Many of the documents were added to the data base by the ERIC Clearinghouse on Adult, Career, and Vocational Education at Ohio State University.

The bibliography is organized into three main sections. The first section presents documents that provide general information, including annotated bibliographies and descriptive, research, and evaluative reports. The second section is composed of titles of manuals and guides that deal primarily with program implementation and administration at both the state and local levels. Modules, which serve as self-instructional devices for teachers, counselors, administrators, and students of occupational education, are covered in the third section. Many of these modules deal with the delivery of competency-based programs.

Most of the ERIC documents listed here are available on microfiche and in paper copy from the ERIC Document Reproduction Service (EDRS), 3900 Wheeler Ave., Alexandria, VA 22304-5510. The microfiche price for documents under 480 pages is $.78. Prices for paper copies are: 1-25 pages, $1.85; 26-50 pages, $3.70; 51-75 pages, $5.55; and 76-100 pages, $7.40; for each additional 25 pages, add $1.85. These prices are subject to change. Postage must be added to all orders. Abstracts of documents in the junior college collection are available upon request from the ERIC Clearinghouse for Junior Colleges, 8118 Math-Sciences Building, University of California, Los Angeles, CA 90024.

A listing of additional sources for curriculum information follows the bibliography. Brief descriptions of organizations, including available services and addresses, are provided.

General Information

Adams, F. G., and Stoyanoff, K. *A Study of Illinois Employer Reactions to Training Credentials.* Grayslake, Ill.: Lake County College, 1982. 62 pp. (ED 227 901)

This study report describes the 1982 Research in Accrediting Efforts Project at Lake County College in Illinois. Interviews of 1,000 urban and rural small-business employers were conducted in an effort to determine their attitudes and beliefs about various forms of accreditation of training among prospective employers. The report includes data tables and survey instruments.

Doty, C. R. *Longitudinal Evaluation of Technical Programs in Community Colleges and Technical Institutes.* 1984. 41 pp. (ED 258 606)

Designed to identify sources for planning longitudinal evaluation strategies, this paper provides an overview and bibliography of resources regarding vocational follow-up and presents a conceptual model for longitudinal program assessment.

Doty, C. R., and DeCastro, C. *Decision Making Systems and Data Sources for Technical Education in Community Colleges/Technical Institutes.* 1984. 46 pp. (ED 258 607)

This annotated bibliography, covering the years 1974-1984, cites sources dealing with two problems: deciding which curricula should be developed and developing curricula efficiently.

Kerstiens, G. *Evaluation of the Policies, Practices and Procedures: Cooperative Career Education Program, El Camino College.* Torrance, Calif.: El Camino College, 1983. 59 pp. (ED 231 450)

This evaluative report assesses the effectiveness of El Camino College's Cooperative Career Education (CCE) program, which awards credit for on-the-job experiential learning related to a student's course of study. The study report includes recommendations for the CCE program's improvement, item-by-item survey responses for each group, and responses to open-ended questions.

Kopecek, R. J., and Clarke, R. G. (eds.). *Customized Job Training for Business and Industry.* New Directions for Community Colleges, no. 48. San Francisco: Jossey-Bass, 1984.

This sourcebook contains eight articles that describe and analyze contracted customized training for business and industry, provided by community colleges. An annotated bibliography of relevant ERIC documents is included.

Leach, J. A., Wentling, T. L., Barnard, W. S., Nash, L. G., and Adams, F. G. *Literature Review with Annotated Bibliography. The Accreditation of Training Experiences: Implications for Employment Training Programs.* Grayslake, Ill.: Lake County College, 1982. 124 pp. (ED 226 812)

This volume reviews the primary methods used or available for use in recording formal training experiences, providing a seventy-seven-item annotated bibliography, which summarizes technical reports, textbooks, journal articles, congressional testimony, final reports, and conference presentations that relate to academic and nonacademic accrediting and to Comprehensive Employment and Training Act system approaches.

Leske, G., and Persico, J., Jr. *Indicators of Quality in Cooperative Vocational Education: A Review and Synthesis of Research.* St. Paul, Minn.: Minnesota Research and Development Center for Vocational Education, 1984. 126 pp. (ED 242 874)

This literature review identifies the major conceptual problems associated with secondary cooperative vocational education (CVE) programs, presents a model that accurately depicts the CVE process, and provides a comprehensive set of measures for quality CVE programs.

Los Angeles Community College District. *Meeting Technical Education Needs: An Industry-Responsive Model. A Supplement.* Los Angeles: Los Angeles Community College District, 1982. 191 pp. (ED 216 721)

This report provides the results of a task-force examination of the status of high-technology programs on the nine campuses of the Los

Angeles Community College District (LACCD) and an exploration of alternative funding possibilities. The report includes the results of faculty and student surveys concerning existing LACCD programs in computer science, electronics, and avionics.

McCormick, R. W. *Vocational-Technical Education Interface with Ohio's High Technology Business and Industrial Sector. Final Report.* Columbus, Ohio: Ohio State Advisory Council for Vocational Education, 1983. 41 pp. (ED 228 416)

This research report presents the findings of personal interviews with thirty-two educators and fifteen industry executives to explore the relationship of vocational-technical educational institutions in Ohio with businesses and industries that apply high technology.

Stoyanoff, K., and Klehm, J. (eds.). *Research in Accrediting Efforts (Project REA). An Assessment on the Awarding of Academic Credit for CETA Activities in Illinois. Case Studies.* Grayslake, Ill.: Lake County College, 1981. 216 pp. (ED 227 914)

This evaluative report reviews fifteen case studies conducted in Illinois Comprehensive Employment and Training Act (CETA) regions. These studies examined the type of credentialing mechanisms used in each region for awarding academic credit and other achievement measures to eligible CETA program participants. The report reviews each of the case studies, providing demographic data, program descriptions, and a discussion of the use of credit mechanisms. Recommendations for follow-up studies are included.

Vocational Special Needs Program. *Resource Guides. Vocational Special Needs Lending Library.* College Station: University of Texas, 1984.

This series of annotated bibliographies describes the collection of the lending library of the Vocational Special Needs Program at Texas A&M University. The guides, which were edited by M. R. Kok, each cover a specific aspect or subject area of the collection. The series includes:

Assessment and Evaluation Materials; 38 pp. (ED 260 259)
Prevocational Instructional Materials; 27 pp. (ED 260 260)
Agricultural Education Materials; 15 pp. (ED 260 261)
Industrial Education Materials; 19 pp. (ED 260 262)
Health Occupations Materials; 14 pp. (ED 260 263)
Employment-Related Instructional Materials; 25 pp. (ED 260 264)
Limited-English Proficiency; 32 pp. (ED 260 265)
Homemaking Materials; 25 pp. (ED 260 267)
Office Education Materials; 14 pp. (ED 260 268)
Marketing and Distributive Education Materials; 19 pp. (ED 260 269)

Warmbrod, C. P., Persavich, J. J., and L'Angelle, D. *Sharing Resources: Postsecondary Education and Industry Cooperation. Research and Development Series No. 203.* Columbus, Ohio: National Center for Research in Vocational Education, 1981. 150 pp. (ED 204 532)

This book contains a descriptive listing of 219 exemplary programs and practices that utilize the sharing concept between postsecondary occupational education and industry, identifying models and guidelines for the sharing of facilities, equipment, materials, and personnel for mutual educational and financial benefit. Guidelines for industry-education cooperation are presented. Appendixes include a report of a needs-sensing workshop, the survey questionnaire that provided information for this book, and a program index.

Handbooks and Guides

Adams, F. G., Stoyanoff, K., Lopez, N., Oen, U., and Willet, L. *Operator's Manual: A Guide for Securing Credentials for Training through Illinois Educational Institutions.* Grayslake, Ill.: Lake County College, 1982. 162 pp. (ED 227 902)

This manual provides guidelines for setting up employment skills training activities for the chronically unemployed, focusing on the establishment of a system to provide credentials for training. The manual provides detailed information on training opportunities, accreditation procedures, and potential linkages for each of six educational sectors: community colleges, secondary schools, regional vocational centers, adult education, proprietary schools, and community-based organizations.

Beilby, A., Edsall, A., Confrey, J., Gomer, A., Harrington, P., Mann, B., and Vitale, P. *Cooperative Education in Two-Year Colleges: Guidelines for Program Development.* Ithaca, N.Y.: Cornell Institute for Occupational Education, 1980. 130 pp. (ED 217 179)

Intended primarily for directors and coordinators of cooperative education at New York's two-year colleges, this guide presents a systematic approach to the development of cooperative education programs and provides means for their review and improvement. Extensive appendixes include an annotated bibliography, discussion of Appalachian Regional Commission and Comprehensive Employment and Training Act funding, suggested curriculum for precooperative courses, and sample forms.

Competency-Based Individualized Vocational Education Consortium. *Self-Instructional Competency-Based Professional Teacher Training Manuals.* Addison, Ill.: Competency-Based Individualized Vocational Education Consortium, 1985.

This series of thirteen self-instructional teacher-training manuals was designed to assist vocational-technical educators and industrial trainers in developing competency-based vocational education (CBVE). These manuals cover approaches to implementation of CBVE, monitoring of student progress, material selection and revision, and maximizing staff and administrative effectiveness. The series includes:

Construct Performance and Written Evaluation Instruments; 78 pp. (ED 261 144)
Write Measurable Performance Objectives; 65 pp. (ED 261 145)
Identify, Verify, and Sequence Job Tasks; 98 pp. (ED 261 146)
Identify the Characteristics of a Competency-Based Vocational Education (CBVE) Program; 54 pp. (ED 261 147)
Develop a Learning Resource Center; 49 pp. (ED 261 157)
Prepare a Staff Development Program; 53 pp. (ED 261 158)
Identify Administrative Support Necessary to Implement CBVE; 21 pp. (ED 261 159)
Assign Grades; 41 pp. (ED 261 160)
Monitor Student Progress and Maintain Student Records; 52 pp. (ED 261 161)
Select and Design Print and Non-Print Resource Materials; 74 pp. (ED 261 162)
Identify Teaching/Learning Strategies and Management Techniques to Implement CBVE; 53 pp. (ED 261 163)
Write Student Learning Guides or Competency Sheets; 119 pp. (ED 261 164)
Adapt or Revise a Student Learning Guide or Competency Sheet; 64 pp. (ED 261 165)
Orient Students to CBVE; 77 pp. (ED 261 166)
Write a Student Performance Contract; 34 pp. (ED 261 167)

Dallas County Community College District. *Cooperative Education Employer's Guide.* Dallas, Tex.: Dallas County Community College District, 1983. 12 pp. (ED 230 209)

Designed for employers in the Dallas County area, this guide provides questions and answers on cooperative education in the Dallas County Community College District. The guide illustrates the steps in the cooperative education process and highlights the benefits of cooperative education for the student, employer, college, and community.

Dallas County Community College District. *Cooperative Education Student Guide.* Dallas, Tex.: Dallas County Community College District, 1982. 21 pp. (ED 227 904)

Designed for students in the Dallas County Community College District's cooperative education program, this guide provides information on obtaining college credit for the development and achievement of learning objectives through current work experience.

Idaho State University. *Idaho Cooperative Education Handbook. An Interdisciplinary Approach for Secondary and Post-Secondary Education.* Pocatello, Idaho: Idaho State University, 1984. 395 pp. (ED 260 270)

This handbook, developed through application of an interdisciplinary approach, is designed as a guide for secondary and postsecondary schools and districts in implementing and administering cooperative education programs in Idaho. The guide contains a variety of forms, letters, charts, and other samples for the teacher-coordinator of cooperative programs.

Kendall, J. C. *A Guide to Environmental Internships: How Environmental Organizations Can Utilize Internships Effectively.* Raleigh, N.C.: National Society for Internships and Experiential Education, 1984. 52 pp. (ED 260 628)

Guidelines based on 1983-1984 interviews and surveys of environmental group representatives are presented for environmental organizations that wish to establish student internships or use interns more effectively.

Maxwell, G. W., and West, L. N. *Handbook for Developing Competency-Based Curricula for New and Emerging Occupations: A Handbook for California Vocational Educators.* San Jose, Calif.: San Jose State University, 1980. 104 pp. (ED 210 518)

This handbook is designed to help vocational educators incorporate changes in the labor market quickly and effectively into their curricula. The handbook is divided into three sections, which guide teachers and administrators through the major steps in developing competency-based curricula for new and emerging technologies: (1) identifying new and emerging occupations; (2) performing task analysis on a new and emerging occupation; and (3) developing competency-based vocational education curricula.

National Center for Research in Vocational Education. *Preparing for High Technology.* Columbus, Ohio: National Center for Research in Vocational Education, 1982.

This series provides information on building collaborative efforts between postsecondary vocational education institutions and businesses and industries that manufacture or employ advanced technology. The series includes:

Preparing for High Technology: Programs That Work; 57 pp. (ED 216 167), which provides case studies of collaborative agreements

Preparing for High Technology: Strategies for Change; 47 pp. (ED 216 168), a research report on technological innovations in telecommunications, computer applications, and advanced manufacturing technologies

Preparing for High Technology: A Guide for Community Colleges; 23 pp. (ED 216 169), which offers guidance on the implementation or improvement of collaborative programs.

National Society for Internships and Experiential Education. *Peer Assistance Network in Experiential Learning (PANEL) Resource Papers.* Raleigh, N.C.: National Society for Internships and Experiential Education, 1981-1983.

The PANEL Resource Paper series provides guides and reports on various aspects of internships and experiential education, primarily at the postsecondary level. Papers cover the history, theory, research, and practice of internship programs and experiential education. The series includes:

History and Rationale for Experiential Learning. PANEL Resource Paper no. 1. 1981. 16 pp. (ED 260 631)

Legal Issues in Experiential Education. PANEL Resource Paper no. 3. 1981. 14 pp. (ED 260 632)

Monitoring and Supporting Experiential Education. PANEL Resource Paper no. 5. 1982. 20 pp. (ED 260 633)

Performance and Appraisal: A Guide to Better Supervisor Evaluation Processes. PANEL Resource Paper no. 7. 1982. 22 pp. (ED 260 634)

Applications of Developmental Theory to the Design and Conduct of Quality Field Experience Programs: Exercises for Educators. PANEL Resource Paper no. 8. 1982. 38 pp. (ED 260 635)

Bibliography of Research in Experiential Learning, Internships and Field Studies. PANEL Resource Paper no. 10. 1983. 28 pp. (ED 260 636)

Environmental Internships: Where Are They and Who Is Wanted? PANEL Resource Paper no. 11. 1983. 18 pp. (ED 260 637)

Experiential Learning and Cultural Models. PANEL Resource Paper no. 12. 1983. 51 pp. (ED 260 638)

Self-Directed Adult Learners and Learning. PANEL Resource Paper no. 13. 1983. 24 pp. (ED 260 639)

Research Agenda for Experiential Education in the 80's. PANEL Resource Paper no. 14. 1984. 33 pp. (ED 260 640)

Oen, U. *Illinois Competency-Based Education Programs and the Employment and Training Community.* Grayslake, Ill.: Lake County College, 1982. 99 pp. (ED 226 811)

Designed for use by employment skills training operators and educators, this descriptive guide provides information on competency-based education (CBE) and its use in Illinois. Appendixes include samples of student competency sheets, learning guides, and evaluation forms; a goal (task) list; a sample certificate; survey materials; and a description of a competency-based individualized vocational education project.

Starr, H., Merz, H., and Zahniser, G. *Using Labor Market Information in Vocational Planning. R & D Series no. 228.* Columbus, Ohio: National Center for Research in Vocational Education, 1982. 108 pp. (ED 216 209)

This guide describes a procedure whereby state and local education agencies can develop long-range program plans for vocational education, placing special emphasis on the numerous ways of utilizing labor market information in program development and evaluation.

Virginia Polytechnic Institute and State University. *Implementing Competency-Based Education in Community Colleges (ICBECC).* Blacksburg: Virginia Polytechnic Institute and State University, 1980.

This series contains ten implementation guides designed primarily for use by instructors. These guides describe the application and maintenance of performance objectives in the classroom, syllabus development, testing and other evaluative techniques, and background materials on the theory and use of performance goals as a teaching strategy. The series includes:

Using Performance Goals: ICBECC 1; 23 pp. (ED 195 299)
Using Performance Objectives: ICBECC 2; 22 pp. (ED 195 300)
Developing a Performance Syllabus: ICBECC 3; 22 pp. (ED 195 301)
Evaluating Performances: ICBECC 4; 31 pp. (ED 195 302)
Motivating Performance Learning: ICBECC 5; 17 pp. (ED 195 303)
Developing and Using Performance Modules: ICBECC 6; 26 pp. (ED 195 304)
Addressing Affective Performance: ICBECC 7; 24 pp. (ED 195 305)
Remediating and Enriching Performance Learning: ICBECC 8; 15 pp. (ED 195 306)
Managing a Performance on the Job: ICBECC 9; 35 pp. (ED 195 307)
Maximizing Teaching/Learning: ICBECC 10; 17 pp. (ED 195 308)

Manuals

American Association for Counseling and Development. *Competency-Based Career Guidance Modules.* Alexandria, Va.: American Association for Counseling and Development, 1985.

This series contains thirty-four competency-based career guidance program training modules organized into five main categories: guidance program planning (six modules); legislative support mechanisms (five modules); program implementation (nineteen modules); operation (two modules); and evaluation (two modules). Patterned after the Performance-Based Teacher Education Modules developed at the National Center for Research in Vocational Education, the modules focus on specific professional and paraprofessional competencies of guidance personnel. The modules are available from Bell and Howell Publications Systems Division, Old Mansfield Rd., Wooster, Ohio 44691. The series includes:

Identify and Plan for Guidance Program Change. Module CG A-1 of Category A—Guidance Program Planning; 54 pp. (ED 257 976)

Organize Guidance Program Development Team. Module CG A-2 of Category A—Guidance Program Planning; 87 pp. (ED 257 977)

Collaborate with the Community. Module CG A-3 of Category A—Guidance Program Planning; 97 pp. (ED 257 978)

Establish a Career Development Theory. Module CG A-4 of Category A—Guidance Program Planning; 90 pp. (ED 257 979)

Build a Guidance Program Planning Model. Module CG A-5 of Category A—Guidance Program Planning; 108 pp. (ED 257 980)

Determine Client and Environmental Needs. Module CG A-6 of Category A—Guidance Program Planning; 64 pp. (ED 257 981)

Influence Legislation. Module CG B-1 of Category B—Supporting; 305 pp. (ED 257 982)

Write Proposals. Module CG B-2 of Category B—Supporting; 74 pp. (ED 257 983)

Improve Public Relations and Community Involvement. Module CG B-3 of Category B—Supporting; 53 pp. (ED 257 984)

Conduct Staff Development Activities. Module CG B-4 of Category B—Supporting; 85 pp. (ED 257 985)

Use and Comply with Administrative Mechanisms. Module CG B-5 of Category B—Supporting; 82 pp. (ED 257 986)

Counsel Individuals and Groups. Module CG C-1 of Category C—Implementing; 78 pp. (ED 257 987)

Tutor Clients. Module CG C-2 of Category C—Implementing; 84 pp. (ED 257 988)

Conduct Computerized Guidance. Module CG C-3 of Category C—Implementing; 48 pp. (ED 257 989)

Infuse Curriculum-Based Guidance. Module CG C-4 of Category C—Implementing; 88 pp. (ED 257 990)

Coordinate Career Resource Centers. Module CG C-5 of Category C—Implementing; 70 pp. (ED 257 991)

Promote Home-Based Guidance. Module CG C-6 of Category C—Implementing; 64 pp. (ED 257 992)

Develop a Work Experience Program. Module CG C-7 of Category C—Implementing; 50 pp. (ED 257 993)

Provide Employability Skill Development. Module CG C-8 of Category C—Implementing; 76 pp. (ED 257 994)

Provide for the Basic Skills. Module CG C-9 of Category C—Implementing; 85 pp. (ED 257 995)

Conduct Placement and Referral Program Activities. Module CG C-10 of Category C—Implementing; 72 pp. (ED 257 996)

Facilitate Follow-Up and Follow-Through. Module CG C-11 of Category C—Implementing; 109 pp. (ED 257 997)

Provide Career Guidance to Girls and Women. Module CG C-13 of Category C—Implementing; 80 pp. (ED 257 998)
Enhance Understanding of Individuals with Disabilities. Module CG C-14 of Category C—Implementing; 77 pp. (ED 257 999)
Help Ethnic Minorities with Career Guidance. Module CG C-15 of Category C—Implementing; 73 pp. (ED 258 000)
Meet Guidance Needs of Older Adults. Module CG C-16 of Category C—Implementing; 88 pp. (ED 258 001)
Promote Equity and Client Advocacy. Module CG C-17 of Category C—Implementing; 48 pp. (ED 258 002)
Assist Clients with Equity Rights and Responsibilities. Module CG C-18 of Category C—Implementing; 152 pp. (ED 258 003)
Develop Ethical and Legal Standards. Module CG C-19 of Category C—Implementing; 56 pp. (ED 258 004)
Ensure Program Operations. Module CG D-1 of Category D—Operating; 57 pp. (ED 258 005)
Aid Professional Growth. Module CG D-2 of Category D—Operating; 83 pp. (ED 258 006)
Evaluate Guidance Activities. Module CG E-1 of Category E—Evaluating; 82 pp. (ED 258 007)
Communicate and Use Evaluation-Based Decisions. Module CG E-2 of Category E—Evaluation; 40 pp. (ED 258 008)

American Institutes for Research in the Behavioral Sciences. *Testing Vocational Education Curriculum Specialist Materials.* American Institutes for Research in the Behavioral Sciences, 1981-1982. (Available from East Central Network Curriculum Center, Sangamon State University, E-22, Springfield, IL 62708; $35.00 for set of 16 modules, an instructor's guide, audiocassette, and field test report. Also available individually.)

This series of documents presents a program designed to train the vocational education curriculum specialist (VECS). The two-part field test report and a descriptive report provide an overview of the program and its modules, which were created to develop or upgrade the curriculum development and management skills of VECS. The sixteen competency-based modules are intended for all instructional settings and teaching methods, with target populations ranging from undergraduate to graduate students and practicing teachers and administrators. The series includes:

Field Testing Vocational Education Curriculum Specialist Materials Summary Abstract. 1981. 19 pp. (ED 215 114)
Field Testing Vocational Education Curriculum Specialist Materials. Final Technical Report. 1981. 35 pp. (ED 215 115)
Adapting Vocational Education to the 80's through Human Resource Development. 1982. 22 pp. (ED 215 116)

Vocational Educators and Curriculum Management. VECS, Module 1. 1981. 37 pp. (ED 215 117)
The Scope of Vocational Education. VECS, Module 2. 1981. 50 pp. (ED 215 118)
Organization of Vocational Education. VECS, Module 3. 1981. 51 pp. (ED 215 119)
Legislative Mandates for Vocational Education. VECS, Module 4. 1981. 55 pp. (ED 215 120)
Priorities in Vocational Education. VECS, Module 5. 1981. 44 pp. (ED 215 121)
Vocational Education for Students with Special Needs. VECS, Module 6. 1981. 69 pp. (ED 215 122)
Vocational Needs Assessment and Curriculum Development. VECS, Module 7. 1981. 78 pp. (ED 215 123)
Conducting Task Analysis and Developing Instructional Objectives. VECS, Module 8. 1981. 73 pp. (ED 215 124)
Selecting Instructional Strategies and Assessing Student Achievement. VECS, Module 9. 1981. 82 pp. (ED 215 125)
Relating Learning Differences and Instructional Methods. VECS, Module 10. 1981. 66 pp. (ED 215 126)
Selecting and Preparing Instructional Materials. VECS, Module 11. 1981. 61 pp. (ED 215 127)
Evaluating Vocational Education Curricula. VECS, Module 12. 1981. 69 pp. (ED 215 128)
Conducting Follow-Up Studies and Communicating Evaluation Results. VECS, Module 13. 1981. 85 pp. (ED 215 129)
Managing Vocational Education Programs. VECS, Module 14. 1981. 59 pp. (ED 215 130)
Preparing for Curriculum Change. VECS, Module 15. 1981. 55 pp. (ED 215 131)
Staff Development. VECS, Module 16. 1981. 57 pp. (ED 215 132)

Center for Continuing Education, University of British Columbia. *Introduction to Teaching Adults.* Vancouver: Center for Continuing Education, University of British Columbia, 1981.

The following modules were designed to meet the learning needs of part-time continuing education instructors. They can also be used as resource materials for local workshops or study-discussion groups, for self-instruction (each module is approximately two hours long), and for a correspondence course. Modules 2-11 were constructed to be used in conjunction with an audiotape. (Paper copies are not available from EDRS. Available from University of British Columbia, Centre Education, 5997 Iona Dr., Vancouver, BC V6T 2A4; $40.00 per set, including cassettes, for Canadian residents; $110.00, plus postage and handling,

international orders; 10 percent discount on ten or more sets.) The series includes:
> *Module 1: Guidelines for Teachers and Adults;* 29 pp. (ED 208 201)
> *Module 2: Using Instructional Techniques;* 27 pp. (ED 208 202)
> *Module 3: Using Instructional Media;* 27 pp. (ED 208 203)
> *Module 4: Using Evaluation Instruments;* 25 pp. (ED 208 204)
> *Module 5: Designing Instruction;* 25 pp. (ED 208 205)
> *Module 6: Writing Instructional Objectives;* 28 pp. (ED 208 206)
> *Module 7: Managing Instruction;* 17 pp. (ED 208 207)
> *Module 8: Enhancing Motivation;* 22 pp. (ED 208 208)
> *Module 9: Understanding the Adult as Learner;* 17 pp. (ED 208 209)
> *Module 10: Understanding the Learning Process;* 21 pp. (ED 208 210)
> *Module 11: Continuing Your Development;* 20 pp. (ED 208 211)

Conserva, Inc. *Apprentice-Related Training Modules* and *Instructor Guides and Training Modules.* Raleigh, N.C.: Conserva, Inc., 1982.

The following group of documents focuses on the first and second years of vocational education apprenticeship programs. A descriptive learner's pamphlet; nine apprentice-related training modules (ARTMS), a series of core instructional materials for the apprentice; and instructor training modules (ITMs) on related subjects of instruction are provided. The series includes:
> *The Role of Vocational Education in Apprenticeship;* 28 pp. (ED 227 282)
> *Introduction to Apprenticeship. ARTM;* 30 pp. (ED 227 283)
> *Working with Organizations. ARTM;* 32 pp. (ED 227 284)
> *Interpersonal Skills and Communication. ARTM;* 39 pp. (ED 227 285)
> *Basic Physical Science. ARTM;* 43 pp. (ED 227 286)
> *Basic Mathematics. ARTM;* 83 pp. (ED 227 287)
> *Basic Measurement. ARTM;* 45 pp. (ED 227 288)
> *Basic Safety I. ARTM;* 38 pp. (ED 227 289)
> *Basic Safety II. ARTM;* 46 pp. (ED 227 290)
> *Sketching, Drawing and Blueprint Reading. ARTM;* 42 pp. (ED 227 291)
> *A Basic Core Curriculum. Instructor's Guide to Apprentice-Related Training Modules;* 19 pp. (ED 227 292)
> *Introduction to Related Subjects Instruction and Inservice Training Materials. ITM no. 1;* 16 pp. (ED 227 293)
> *Planning the Apprenticeship Program. ITM no. 2.* 45 pp. (ED 227 294)
> *Planning Related Subjects Instruction. ITM no. 3;* 33 pp. (ED 227 295)
> *Developing Instructional Materials for Apprentices. ITM no. 4;* 41 pp. (ED 227 296)

Presenting Information. ITM no. 5; 34 pp. (ED 227 297)
Directing Learning Activities for Instruction. ITM no. 6; 37 pp. (ED 227 298)
Providing for Individual Learner Needs. ITM no. 7; 35 pp. (ED 227 299)
Controlling Instructional Settings. ITM no. 8; 27 pp. (ED 227 300)
Evaluating Apprentice Performance. ITM no. 9; 36 pp. (ED 227 301)
Communicating with Apprentices. ITM no. 10; 37 pp. (ED 227 302)

National Center for Research in Vocational Education. *Competency-Based Vocational Education Administrator Module Series.* Columbus, Ohio: National Center for Research in Vocational Education, 1983.

These four competency-based administrator education learning modules focus on specific professional competencies needed by vocational education administrators. Each package is designed to be used by administrators or prospective administrators working individually or in groups under the direction of a resource person. (Available from American Association for Vocational Instructional Materials, 120 Driftmier Engineering Center, University of Georgia, Athens, GA 30602.) The series includes:

Direct Curriculum Development. Module LT-B-1 of Category B—Instructional Management; 72 pp. (ED 236 383)
Manage Student Recruitment. Module LT-C-1 of Category C—Student Services; 92 pp. (ED 236 384)
Supervise Vocational Education Personnel (Rev. ed.). Module LT-D-2 of Category D—Personnel Management; 59 pp. (ED 236 385)
Promote the Vocational Education Program. Module LT-F-2 of Category F—School-Community Relations; 109 pp. (ED 236 386)

National Center for Research in Vocational Education. *Professional Teacher Education Module Series.* Columbus, Ohio: National Center for Research in Vocational Education, 1985. (Available from American Association for Vocational Instructional Materials, 120 Driftmier Engineering Center, University of Georgia, Athens, GA 30602.)

The following are revised and new modules in a series of more than 125 performance-based teacher education learning packages focusing on specific professional competencies of vocational instructors. The modules are designed for the preparation of instructors in all occupational areas. The series contains:

Maintain an Occupational Advisory Committee (2d ed.). Module A-5 of Category A—Program Planning, Development, and Evaluation; 38 pp. (ED 255 669)
Conduct an Occupational Analysis (2d ed.). Module A-7 of Category A—Program Planning, Development, and Evaluation; 77 pp. (ED 260 271)

Develop a Course of Study (2d ed.). Module A-8 of Category A—Program Planning, Development, and Evaluation; 49 pp. (ED 259 134)

Develop a Unit of Instruction (2d ed.). Module B-3 of Category B—Instructional Planning; 55 pp. (ED 240 382)

Develop a Lesson Plan (2d ed.). Module B-4 of Category B—Instructional Planning; 36 pp. (ED 240 314)

Employ Brainstorming, Buzz Group, and Question Box Techniques (2d ed.). Module C-3 of Category C—Instructional Execution; 28 pp. (ED 244 136)

Direct Student Laboratory Experience (2d ed.). Module C-7 of Category C—Instructional Execution; 60 pp. (ED 246 306)

Employ Oral Questioning Techniques (2d ed.). Module C-12 of Category C—Instructional Execution; 44 pp. (ED 245 075)

Demonstrate a Manipulative Skill (2d ed.). Module C-16 of Category C—Instructional Execution; 40 pp. (ED 236 356)

Establish Student Performance Criteria (2d ed.). Module D-1 of Category D—Instructional Evaluation; 29 pp. (ED 259 205)

Assess Student Performance: Knowledge (2d ed.). Module D-2 of Category D—Instructional Evaluation; 71 pp. (ED 240 313)

Assess Student Performance: Attitudes (2d ed.). Module D-3 of Category D—Instructional Evaluation; 37 pp. (ED 242 951)

Assess Student Performance: Skills (2d ed.). Module D-4 of Category D—Instructional Evaluation; 32 pp. (ED 234 161)

Determine Student Grades (2d ed.). Module D-5 of Category D—Instructional Evaluation; 41 pp. (ED 242 952)

Establish Guidelines for Your Cooperative Vocational Program (2d ed.). Module J-1 of Category J—Coordination of Cooperative Education; 45 pp. (ED 262 204)

Prepare Yourself for CBE. Module K-1 of Category K—Implementing Competency-Based Education (CBE); 67 pp. (ED 262 292)

Organize the Content for a CBE Program. Module K-2 of Category K—Implementing Competency-Based Education (CBE); 61 pp. (ED 266 275)

Organize Your Class and Lab to Install CBE. Module K-3 of Category K—Implementing Competency-Based Education (CBE); 78 pp. (ED 266 276)

Provide Instructional Materials for CBE. Module K-4 of Category K—Implementing Competency-Based Education (CBE); 62 pp. (ED 266 277)

Manage the Daily Routines of Your CBE Program. Module K-5 of Category K—Implementing Competency-Based Education (CBE); 61 pp. (ED 266 278)

Guide Your Students through the CBE Program. Module K-6 of Category K—Implementing Competency-Based Education (CBE); 54 pp. (ED 266 279)

Norton, R. E., Harrington, L. G., and Fardig, G. E. *Develop and Implement a Competency-Based Education Program. Module CBE-1.* Columbus, Ohio: National Postsecondary Alliance, 1980. 171 pp. (ED 237 141)

This module contains 11 sequential learning experiences designed to provide educators with background information and opportunities to develop plans for implementing competency-based education (CBE) programs within their institutions. Each of the eleven units includes enabling objectives, activities to assist in objective fulfillment, and feedback devices.

Additional Sources of Up-to-Date Curriculum Information

Open Entries. Open Entries is a quarterly publication that provides educators with an information system for the exchange of competency-based instructional materials and methodologies. For a subscription, contact *Open Entries,* The Center for Studies in Vocational Education, Stone Building, Tallahassee, FL 32306.

The National Curriculum Network. The National Curriculum Network consists of six regional centers that provide free computer searches of ERIC and other data bases. The network's primary data base is VECM (Vocational Education Curriculum Materials), in which microcomputer courseware, workbooks, modules, and audiovisual materials are available. Contact the center nearest your institution for a complete description of services available.

East Central
Sangamon State University
Springfield, IL 62708
(217) 786-6375

Midwest
1515 West Sixth Ave.
Stillwater, OK 74074
(405) 377-2000

Northeast
Rutgers–The State University of New Jersey
Crest Way
Aberdeen, NJ 07747
(201) 290-1900

Northwest
Saint Martin's College
Old Main Building, R474
Lacey, WA 98503
(206) 438-4456

Southeast
Mississippi State University
Drawer DX
Mississippi State, MS 39762
(601) 325-2510

Western
University of Hawaii at Manoa
1776 University Ave.
Honolulu, HI 98622
(808) 948-7834

The Vocational Technical Education Consortium of States (VTECS). VTECS specializes in competency-based vocational-technical education. VTECS produces and periodically revises catalogues that contain job analyses with performance-based goals and objectives. Newly developed catalogues include *Computer Service and Repair Technician, Laser Technician,* and *Robotics Technician.* Emerging occupations are the focus of VTECS's developmental effort. Catalogues are available from VTECS, Southern Association of Colleges and Schools, 795 Peach St. N.E., Atlanta, GA 30365.

The Center for Occupational Research and Development (CORD). CORD is a nonprofit corporation that conducts research, development, evaluation, and dissemination activities in postsecondary education and training for technical occupations. CORD identifies work-force needs in new and expanding occupations and develops program plans and instructional materials for specialized training programs. *The Unified Technical Concepts: Scientific Foundations for High Technical Programs* is a CORD publication. For more information, contact CORD, 601C Lake Air Dr., Waco, TX 76710.

The DACUM Exchange. DACUM (Develop a Curriculum) is a method of occupational analysis in which employers and supervisors identify and analyze the duties of jobs within their fields. The DACUM Exchange provides, at cost, DACUM charts for many occupations. DACUM charts place the duties of a job, with corresponding tasks for each duty, on a time line (for example, charting from the first day on the job to the end of the second year). The DACUM Exchange is at Humber College of Applied Arts and Technology, 205 Humber College Boulevard, Etobicoke, Ontario, Canada M9W 5L7.

Cooperative Education Centers

National Commission for Cooperative Education
360 Huntington Ave.
Boston, MA 02115
(617) 437-3778

National Community College Center for Cooperative Education
Chicago City-Wide College
30 East Lake St.
Chicago, IL 60601
(312) 781-9430

National Society for Internships and Experiential Education (NSIEE)
122 St. Mary's St., 2nd Floor
Raleigh, NC 27605
(919) 834-7536

Associations. The following four professional associations are involved in occupational education in community colleges and technical institutes:

American Technical Education Association
North Dakota School of Science
800 College St.
Wahpeton, ND 58075

National Association of Industrial and Technical Teacher Educators
Department of Occupational Education
Box 7801
North Carolina State University
Raleigh, NC 27695-7801
(N. A. Foell)

American Vocational Association
Technical Education Division
State Technical Institute
Memphis, TN 38134
(J. Van Dyke, Dir. of Development)

National Council for Occupational Education
North Central Technical Institute
1000 Campus Dr.
Wausau, WI 54401
(R. C. Paulsen)

Charles R. Doty is the adviser in technical education at the Graduate School of Education, Rutgers, State University of New Jersey.

Mary P. Hardy is a staff writer at the ERIC Clearinghouse for Junior Colleges, University of California, Los Angeles.

Index

A

Accreditation, 2; classifications for, 38; process of, 36; regional institutional bodies for, 36-38; self-study in, 39-43; site visit in, 43-44
Adams, F. G., 88, 89, 91
Advanced placement programs, 59
Advisory committees: in curriculum development, 10-12; as resource for needs analysis, 32
American Association of Bible Colleges, 37
American Association of Community and Junior Colleges (AACJC), 65, 74; policy on general education, 66-67
American Association for Counseling and Development, 95-97
American Electrologist Association, 51
American Institute of Planners, 51
American Institutes for Research in the Behavioral Sciences, 97
American Medical Association (AMA), 49
American Ophthalmic Society, 50
American Technical Education Association, 104
American Vocational Association, 104
Anderson, W., 10, 22
Appel, M., 30, 32
Arnold, J. P., 2, 57, 64
Arns, K. F., 1, 3
Articulation, 2, 57-58, 63; benefits of, 58; in curriculum development, 16-17; types of, 58-59; typical activities and strategies for, 59-63
Association of Independent Schools and Colleges, 37
Atkin, J. M., 5, 8
Ayres, M. C., 2, 9, 23

B

Barnard, W. S., 89
Beilby, A., 91
Bender, L. W., 67, 75
Brawer, F., 67, 69, 74
British Columbia, University of: Center for Continuing Education, 98-99
Bronowski, J., 1, 3
Bushnell, D. S., 66, 74
Business Week, 28

C

California Department of Consumer Affairs, 52, 56
Callahan, W. V., 10, 12, 15, 22
Campbell, D. F., 2, 65, 68, 69, 74, 75
Careers Tomorrow: The Outlook for Work in a Changing World, 30
Carl D. Perkins Vocational Act, 5. See also Title IV
Casey, K., 2, 3
Catonsville Community College, 72, 74
Center for Occupational Research and Development (CORD), 6-7, 103
Certification, 2, 50; contrasted to licensing, 49-51. See also Recertification; Tests, occupational
Cetron, M., 30, 32
Change: in secondary school curricula, 1; in work force, 1
Clark, D. E., 28, 33
Clarke, R. G., 89
Cohen, A. M., 67, 69, 74
College Level Academic Skills Test (CLAST), 67
Colleges, community: evaluating occupational programs of, 77-85; federal government and curriculum of, 5-8; general education in, 67-73. See also Articulation
Colleges, four-year: articulation with, 16-17; occupational programs in, 68-69
Collins, C. C., 72, 74
Competency-Based Individualized Vocational Education Consortium, 91-92

107

Comprehensive Employment and Training Act (CETA), 90
Confrey, J., 91
Conserva, Inc., 99-100
Cooperative education centers, 104
Cooperative vocational education (CVE) programs, 89
Core programs, 59
Council on Postsecondary Accreditation (COPA), 36, 39, 45
Crane's Chicago Business, 28
Curriculum: applied arts, 1; current policies on, 7; federal government and technical, 5-8; general education in, 66-67
Curriculum development, 2; overview of, 11; process for, 9-22
Curriculum, occupational: bibliography of ERIC information on, 87-102; general education in, 65-74; reasons for studying, 1-2; sources of information on, 102-104

D

DACUM (Develop a Curriculum) Exchange, 103
Dallas County Community College District (DCCCD), 92; occupational program evaluation at, 77-85
Data: on changing labor market, 2, 26-32; from ERIC, 87-102; for feasibility study, 12, 14-15; for occupational program evaluation, 78-79
DeCastro, C., 88
Denison, R. H., 60, 64
Dictionary of Occupational Titles, 14
Doty, C. R., 3, 21, 22, 62, 64, 87, 88, 105
Dun & Bradstreet Corporation, 31

E

Echord, B. S., 3, 77, 86
Edsall, A., 91
Education, 8
Education, general, 2; merging, and occupational education, 67-70; new approaches to, 70-73; in occupational curriculum, 65-66; renewed emphasis on, 66-67; suggestions for future of, 73

Educational Resources Information Center (ERIC): bibliography of occupational program information from, 88-102; obtaining documents from, 88
El Camino College, 89
Electrical Utilities Technical Education Council, 6-7
Employment: in future, 29-30; using projections for, in needs analysis, 27-28
Employment and Earnings, 26
Environmental Protection Agency, 7
Evaluation: of occupational programs, 3, 77-85; of programs in New Jersey, 21-22

F

Fardig, G. E., 102
Feasibility study, in curriculum development, 12-15
Federal Trade Commission, 50
Feingold, N., 30, 32
Feldman, B., 17, 18, 22
Fife, T., 72, 74
Florida, 48-49
Fortune, J. C., 52, 56
Fullerton, H. N., Jr., 29, 32
Furtado, L., 21, 23
Futurist, The, 30

G

Gellhorn, W., 48, 56
General education. *See* Education, general
Gomer, A., 91
Government, federal: publications for needs analysis, 29; and technical curriculum development, 2, 5-8
Grede, J. F., 66, 74
Grimm, K. L., 49, 56
Grubb, W., 9, 12, 22

H

Hagerstown Junior College, 12, 22
Halyard, R. A., 66, 74
Hamel, D. B., 44, 45
Hardy, M. P., 87, 105
Harrington, L. G., 102

Harrington, P., 91
Harris, N. C., 66, 74
Harris Publishing Company, 31
Harvard Committee, 1, 3
Health care, employment in, 28
High Technology, 28
Holcomb, R., 10, 12, 15, 22
House, E. R., 5, 8
Hull, D. M., 6, 8

I

Idaho State University, 93
Illinois, 48-49; new industry monitoring in, 31

J

James Sprunt Community College, 71-72, 73
Jester, A., 73, 74
Joint Commission on Vocational and Technical Education, 58, 64
Justin, M. J., 66, 74

K

Kahl, A., 28, 33
Kekke, R., 74
Kells, H. R., 39, 45
Kendall, J. C., 93
Kentucky, University of, 72
Kerstiens, G., 89
Kirkwood Community College, 72, 74
Klehm, J., 90
Kopecek, R. J., 89
Korim, A. S., 68, 69, 74

L

L'Angelle, D., 91
Lake County College, 88
Laser/electro-optics technology (LEOT) project, 6
Leach, J. A., 89
Leske, G., 89
Licensure, 2, 50; contrasted to certification, 49-51. *See also* Relicensure; Tests, occupational
Long, J. P., 59, 64
Lopez, N., 91
Los Angeles Community College District, 89-90
Los Medanos College, 72
Lukasiewicz, J. M., 28, 33
Lukenbill, J. D., 71, 74

M

McCabe, R. H., 71, 74
McCormick, R. W., 90
Mahoney, J. R., 66, 74
Mann, B., 91
Manufacturers' News, Inc., 31
Manufacturing, 2
Martinez, T., Jr., 3, 77, 86
Maxwell, G. W., 93
Merz, H., 95
Miami-Dade Community College, general education program, 70-71
Middle States Association of Colleges and Schools, 36
Miller, N., 30, 32
Minority Business Today, 29
Monthly Labor Review, 26, 29
Morris, W., 10, 12, 15, 22
Murphy, N., 66, 74

N

Nash, L. G., 89
Nasman, L. O., 60, 64
National Association of Industrial and Technical Teacher Educators, 104
National Association of Trade and Technical Schools, 37, 39
National Center for Research in Vocational Education, 7, 93, 100-102
National Commission for Cooperative Education, 104
National Community College Center for Cooperative Education, 104
National Council for Occupational Education, 65, 104; Task Force on the Associate in Applied Science Degree, 67, 75
National Curriculum Network, 102-103
National Endowment for the Humanities, 71, 72
National Home Study Council, 38
National Institute for Automotive Service Excellence, 52
National Institutes of Health, 7

National Occupational Information Coordinating Council, 7
National Oceanic and Atmospheric Administration, 7
National Society for Internships and Experiential Education (NSIEE), 94, 104
National Trade & Professional Associations of the United States Director, 30
Nealon, J. G., 1, 5, 8
Needs analysis, resources for, 25-32
New England Association of Schools and Colleges, 36
New Jersey, program for curriculum development, 9-22
News, 2
Newspapers, for needs analysis, 28-29
North Central Association of Colleges and Schools, 37
Northwest Association of Schools and Colleges, 37, 39, 45
Norton, R. E., 102

O

O'Banion, T., 68, 74
Occupational curriculum. *See* Curriculum, occupational
Occupational tests. *See* Tests, occupational
Occupational Outlook Handbook, 14
Occupations, categories of, 29-30
Oen, U., 91, 94
Ohio Council on Vocational Education, 61, 64
Ohio Department of Education, statistics on vocational education, 58
Open Entries, 102

P

Paris, K. A., 77, 86
Parker, G. G., 66, 74
Parnell, D., 59, 64
Pellaton, J., 54, 56
Periodicals, for needs analysis, 28
Persavich, J. J., 91
Persico, J., Jr., 89
Petry, J. P., 58, 62, 64
Pilot, M., 28, 33
Porter, G. H., 67, 75

Posner, G., 15, 23
Pretech programs, 59
Professional Picture Framers of America, 51
Projections, as resource for needs analysis, 30-31
Public Law 98-524, 7, 10

Q

Quigley, R., 74

R

Raulf, J. F., 2, 9, 23
Rayack, E., 48, 56
Recertification, 51-52
Relicensure, 51-52
Roueche, J. E., 70, 75
Roueche, S. D., 70, 75
Rowe, D., 73
Rowe, F. A., Jr., 72, 75

S

Sagen, H. B., 66, 75
Schools, secondary: articulation with, 16-17; changes in curriculum of, 1; occupational students in, 57-58
Schools, vocational: articulation with, 16-17
Schroeder, B., 21, 23
Schuman, C. C., 1, 3
Self-study: and accreditation, 39-40, 41; for initial accreditation, 41-43; for reaccreditation, 40-41
Shaw, R. G., 68, 74
Shimberg, B., 48, 49, 50, 51, 52, 56
Silvestri, G. T., 28, 33
Site visit, and accreditation, 43-44
Smith, D. B., 2, 25, 33
Southern Association of Colleges and Schools, 37; Commission on Colleges, 67
Standard Industrial Classification (SIC) code, 31-32
Starr, H., 95
Sterling, G., 58, 64
Stoodley, R. V., Jr., 2, 35, 44, 45
Stoyanoff, K., 88, 90, 91
Surveys, industrial: sources for, 31-32

T

Technical Education Research Center (TERC), 5-7
Teryek, C. J., 2, 47, 56
Tests, general education, 67
Tests, occupational, 2; history of, 47-49; preparing for, 54-56; types of, 52-54
Texas A&M University, 90
Thorndike, R. L., 54, 56
Title IV, 5, 7

U

Unemployment, figures on, for needs analysis, 26-27
Unified Technical Concepts: Scientific Foundations for High Technical Programs, The, 103
U.S. Department of Commerce, 29
U.S. Department of Education, 5; and accreditation, 36; policy on national curriculum, 7
U.S. Department of Health, Education, and Welfare, 50, 56
U.S. Department of Health and Human Services, 7
U.S. Department of Justice, 50
U.S. Department of Labor, 50; Bureau of Labor Statistics, 26-27, 29
U.S. Food and Drug Administation, 49
U.S. Government Regional Bookstore, 29

V

Vincent, W., 16, 23
Virginia Polytechnic Institute and State University, 95
Vitale, P., 91
Vocational Education Act: of 1963, 5; of 1976, 10
Vocational Education Curriculum Materials (VECM), 102
Vocational education curriculum specialist (VECS), 97-98
Vocational Special Needs Program, 90
Vocational Technical Education Consortium of States (VTECS), 103

W

Warmbrod, C. P., 91
Weber, J. M., 60, 64
Wentling, T. L., 89
West, L. N., 93
Western Association of Schools and Colleges, 37
Willet, L., 91
Wood, M. T., 2, 65, 75
Work force: changes in, 1; obtaining data on, 26-32
World Future Society, 30

Z

Zahniser, G., 95
Zenger, S., 15, 23
Zenger, W., 15, 23